KT-556-266

NEW PENGUIN SHAKESPEARE

GENERAL EDITOR: T. J. B. SPENCER

ASSOCIATE EDITOR: STANLEY WELLS

WILLIAM SHAKESPEARE

*

MUCH ADO
ABOUT NOTHING

EDITED BY
R. A. FOAKES

PENGUIN BOOKS

PENGUIN BOOKS

Published by the Penguin Group
Penguin Books Ltd, 27 Wrights Lane, London W8 5TZ, England
Penguin Putnam Inc., 375 Hudson Street, New York, New York 10014, USA
Penguin Books Australia Ltd, Ringwood, Victoria, Australia
Penguin Books Canada Ltd, 10 Alcorn Avenue, Toronto, Ontario, Canada M4V 3B2
Penguin Books (NZ) Ltd, Private Bag 102902, NSMC, Auckland, New Zealand

Penguin Books Ltd, Registered Offices: Harmondsworth, Middlesex, England

This edition first published in Penguin Books 1968
Reprinted with revised Further Reading 1996
5 7 9 10 8 6 4

This edition copyright © Penguin Books, 1968, 1996
Introduction and notes copyright © R. A. Foakes, 1968
Further Reading copyright © Michael Taylor, 1996
All rights reserved

Printed in England by Clays Ltd, St Ives plc
Set in Monotype Ehrhardt

CONTENTS

INTRODUCTION

ONLY two performances of *Much Ado About Nothing* within Shakespeare's lifetime are recorded, both at court in 1613, as part of the festivities associated with the marriage of Princess Elizabeth to the Elector Palatine, Prince Frederick (of Bohemia). At one of these the play was called 'Benedicke and Betteris', a title King Charles I also preferred, for he entered it in his copy of Shakespeare's plays, so confirming the impression given by Leonard Digges, in his commendatory verses prefaced to Shakespeare's *Poems* (1640), that, for cultured audiences at any rate, these characters stole the play:

> *let but Beatrice*
> *And Benedick be seen, lo in a trice*
> *The Cockpit galleries, boxes, all are full.*

This has been true almost ever since, for with the exception of a period of sixty years after the restoration of Charles II in 1660, when the play was adapted in various versions, it has been popular on the stage, and leading actors and actresses, from David Garrick and Mrs Pritchard in the eighteenth century to John Gielgud and Peggy Ashcroft in the twentieth, have played Benedick and Beatrice with notable success.

At first glance it may seem odd that these two characters should so dominate a play in which the main 'ado' concerns Don John's villainous attempt to thwart the marriage arranged between Claudio and Hero; but clearly Shakespeare planned it this way, and it is important therefore to

7

try to understand how and why the action turns for any audience on the relations of Beatrice and Benedick. Much has been said about their wit, and it is true that they are more consistently and outrageously witty than others in a play in which the dialogue crackles with repartee. Yet some part of their skirmishes of wit has lost its force over the years; these are often bawdy, and dependent on sexual innuendoes that no longer have effect, like the jokes about cuckolds' horns (see, for example, I.1.222–4), the easy allusions to legends not now so familiar, to Cupid, Vulcan, Hercules, or Prester John, or the word-play drawn from terms used in hunting or fencing. Perhaps it is not so much the quality of their witty exchanges that makes them such powerful and vibrant figures, as the energy and skill with which they parry each other, and so preserve a stance of tough-minded independence.

The world they inhabit, the world of the play, presents itself in the opening scene as a courtly society of Messina awaiting a visit by the Prince of Aragon; but the ostensible scene matters perhaps less in this play than in any of Shakespeare's other comedies. Most of the play is written in prose, and the easy flow of the dialogue establishes a conversational realism that speaks home at once to us. Its atmosphere is very different from that created by the poetic lushness and romantic ardours of Illyria or the Forest of Arden; in *Much Ado* Benedick and Beatrice all the time, and all the court characters at some time, speak with the grace, freedom, and ease of the finest conversation among social equals, who feel free to say what they please to one another; Benedick and Beatrice are recognized and applauded by the others in this highly civilized group of figures as supreme in the 'merry war' of wit, as the cleverest talkers in a society which values their dexterity.

The conversation in this society is realistic in the sense

that it appears to flow spontaneously, as though its happiest jests and quibbles arise naturally from the narrative context, and are not worked in as formal devices; so it is, for example, with Beatrice's clever joke on 'civil' – 'Seville', the Seville orange being sour, and yellow-orange the colour of jealousy:

DON PEDRO *Come, lady, come; you have lost the heart of Signor Benedick.*

BEATRICE *Indeed, my lord, he lent it me awhile, and I gave him use for it, a double heart for his single one. Marry, once before he won it of me with false dice, therefore your grace may well say I have lost it.*

DON PEDRO *You have put him down, lady, you have put him down.*

BEATRICE *So I would not he should do me, my lord, lest I should prove the mother of fools. I have brought Count Claudio, whom you sent me to seek.*

DON PEDRO *Why, how now, Count! Wherefore are you sad?*

CLAUDIO *Not sad, my lord.*

DON PEDRO *How then? Sick?*

CLAUDIO *Neither, my lord.*

BEATRICE *The Count is neither sad, nor sick, nor merry, nor well; but civil count, civil as an orange, and something of that jealous complexion.*   II.1.253–71

Here Beatrice has been asked to fetch Claudio, who thinks Don Pedro has betrayed his trust and wooed Hero for himself. The poise with which Beatrice accepts the loss of 'the heart of Signor Benedick' contrasts with Claudio's sullenness at the idea of losing Hero, and she sharply observes the true origin of his ill-humour in her joke about him. The whole dialogue stems appropriately from the occasion, and Beatrice's quibble brings out what is important for the play's developing action, the jealous disposition of Claudio.

Within this realistic dimension of the play, this natural flow of good talk, Beatrice and Benedick excel by virtue of their intelligence and vitality, and the other characters allow them this supremacy. It is the source of their immediate appeal to readers and audiences. But it would be a mistake to think of them as 'real', and somehow opposed to 'romantic' figures like Claudio and Hero. They belong, with all the court-figures in the play, to a stylized, highly conventional world in which the mundane needs of everyday life fade into the background, no one has to earn a living, the wars are over, and, Don John excepted, all may devote themselves to revelry, and to match-making. In such a world, demure daughters find their mates in accordance with their rank and fortune, and if the match is not arranged by their parents in the normal way, the lovers win through to parental blessing and harmony in the end. Hero belongs to such a pattern, but Beatrice and Benedick seem superior to it, as if their intelligence and vigour enable them to flout conventions, and thus within the play's 'realism' they stand out as more realistic than others.

They are able to flout conventions too because Shakespeare has taken care not to encumber them with close relatives; Benedick has none, and Beatrice is an orphan to whom Leonato, her uncle and guardian (II.3.167) allows a freedom he would not permit his daughter Hero to have. Beatrice talks with a man's licence, and Benedick with the liberty of an independent visitor, the more readily in that there is no one to restrain either of them; and the rest accept this presumption on the part of the young in homage to their superior wit. The supremacy of intelligence, or wit, in the values of the world of the play helps to account for both its brilliance, and its prose. The brilliance is achieved centrally in Beatrice and Benedick, but a price is paid for it; there is a coolness about the gaiety of this world, where to score a point in conversation matters most. However diverting and splendid the two central figures are, they do not arouse in an audience the warmth of feeling accorded a Rosalind or a Portia.

The character in *Much Ado About Nothing* who might conceivably do this is Hero, but to some the presentation of her and of Claudio has seemed a flaw in the play, because they do not sufficiently engage our sympathies. This is to ask for a different kind of play from the one we have; for, given the high valuation put on wit, on sharpness of intelligence, Hero is bound to appear a little stupid, and Claudio too somewhat imperceptive. The contrast between them and Beatrice and Benedick was surely designed in part to expose the limitations of both couples, and Hero and Claudio are shown up as conventional and prim, where in a more straightforwardly 'romantic' play these aspects might have passed unnoticed. In a different way, Beatrice and Benedick are exposed too, the mockers mocked, when they are brought to feel 'little Cupid's crafty arrow', and yield a triumph to heart over mind.

In this festive courtly society, which is relieved of the necessity of doing anything but dance, play, and make schemes for matrimony, maids and young bachelors need to have defences to protect themselves against the wrong kinds of pressure. Beatrice and Benedick have their sharp tongues, which scare fools away, and preserve them as individualists from the need to conform to society's usual arrangements; so Beatrice, who has no father to please, can mock at Hero's obedience:

> *it is my cousin's duty to make curtsy and say, 'Father, as it please you'. But yet for all that, cousin, let him be a handsome fellow, or else make another curtsy and say, 'Father, as it please me'.* II.i.46–9

Hero and Claudio fit into the norm, in so far as their love
springs from the eye, not the mind, as Claudio says to Don
Pedro:

> O, my lord,
> When you went onward on this ended action,
> I looked upon her with a soldier's eye,
> That liked, but had a rougher task in hand
> Than to drive liking to the name of love;
> But now I am returned and that war-thoughts
> Have left their places vacant, in their rooms
> Come thronging soft and delicate desires,
> All prompting me how fair young Hero is,
> Saying I liked her ere I went to wars.   I.i.275–84

Don Pedro woos on Claudio's behalf, and wins the lady,
off stage. The whole thing depends not merely on Hero,
but on the permission of her father, whose duty it is to take
stock of Claudio as husband, and on satisfactory financial
arrangements – Claudio makes sure Hero is Leonato's heir.
Some have argued that their sole concern is social position,
and certainly Claudio has an eye to his future wealth and
status; but this is the way of the world, and also the way of
prudence. His love may be real enough notwithstanding.

Hero and Claudio play the game of love by society's
normal rules; they make arrangements through intermediaries, on whom they rely for advice and protection –
Hero on her father, Claudio on Don Pedro. The young
warrior, returning from the fray, is drawn to Hero for her
beauty; just as Troilus looked on Cressida and discovered

> that Love hadde his dwellynge
> Withinne the subtile stremes of hir yen;
> That sodeynly hym thoughte he felte dyen,
> Right with hire look, the spirit in his herte.
> Blissed be Love, that kan thus folk converte!
>   Chaucer, Troilus and Criseyde I, 304–8

The eye is arbiter, and they love at sight. The guarantee of parents or friends brings judgement into play, and tempers ardour with common sense; but when the game is played by these rules, the parties in it are subject to trickery and deception, simply because the lovers do not know each other fully.

Beatrice and Benedick play by other rules, and like less with the eye than with the mind, relying on their own judgement, not on society's customs. Their wit is not merely a weapon of offence, it is also a means of displaying themselves, what they are, to the world. For all their posing, represented in Benedick's resolve to 'live a bachelor' (I.1.227), and in Beatrice's boast, 'I had rather hear my dog bark at a crow than a man swear he loves me' (I.1.123-4), they are showing themselves off as a preparation for mating, and for ensuring that intelligence matches with intelligence. This is made clear in their preoccupation with each other from the start, and the way in which they talk about each other when they are not speaking together. When Benedick is invited to praise Hero, he talks instead of the beauty of Beatrice (I.1.177-80), and when Beatrice criticizes Don John, she cannot help comparing him with Benedick (II.1.6-7). The tricks practised on them to make them fall in love merely bring into the open what is already implicit in their attention to each other. The power of their love is recognized by them, and by the audience, only when Beatrice calls on Benedick to defend the honour of her friend Hero, and he breaks the ties of friendship with Claudio to accept her mission and 'Kill Claudio' (IV.1.285). In the end they agree together, in terms of an honourable draw as one individual with another; the terms are their own, not those of society, which commonly requires the subjection of women to parents and husbands.

*

Comedy ends with marriage, which brings burdens and responsibilities; the delights and trials of courtship are matter for comedy. Beatrice and Benedick suggest the delights of courtship in their freedom from the curbs usually imposed on the young by society. A different aspect is seen in the story of Hero and Claudio, who belong to the tradition of romance in which lovers endure misfortunes and tribulations before winning through to happiness at the end; and Hero conforms to the pattern in being the embodiment of innocent and simple beauty. Shakespeare invented Benedick and Beatrice, but Claudio and Hero he borrowed from a tale with a very long history stretching back to an ancient Greek romance. Of the numerous versions of this story, Shakespeare seems to have known two in particular, that presented by Ariosto in the fifth canto of *Orlando Furioso* (1516), which was translated by Sir John Harington into English (1591), and the variant narrated by Matteo Bandello in the twenty-second of his *Novelle* (1554); this was translated into French in François de Belleforest's *Histoires Tragiques* (1574), but not into English, so far as is known, during Shakespeare's lifetime. Shakespeare was not the first English author to use the tale for his own purposes; Edmund Spenser included a version in his *Faerie Queene* (1590), Book II, canto IV; George Whetstone printed another account in his miscellany, *The Rock of Regard* (1576), and it formed the basis of a play, *Fedele and Fortunio*, translated from the Italian of Luigi Pasqualigo and printed in 1585.

Shakespeare took over a tale that was already fairly well known in England, and characteristically wove strands from different versions together into a quite new and individual rendering. He took some character-names, notably Don Pedro and Leonato, and the setting, Messina, from Bandello, together with the main outlines of the story. However, in Bandello's story, Timbreo (the Claudio figure) is described as a lord whose rank and wealth far exceed those of Fenicia (the Hero figure), who comes of an ancient, but impoverished, family; his first thought is to seduce her, and his concern later over demeaning himself by marrying her establishes an element of inner conflict in the character. Merely on the sight of someone entering, as he supposes, Fenicia's chamber, Timbreo swells with righteous anger, and demands no more proof, but repudiates her at once. Shakespeare modifies these elements in Bandello's version in such a way as to remove all inner conflict from Claudio. He presents Hero and Claudio as apparently of the same rank, and untroubled by disparity of fortune; and, like the wandering Knight Ariodante in Ariosto's account, Claudio seeks Hero's hand out of mere love, if not quite with Ariodante's romantic ardour.

Moreover, Shakespeare makes the evidence of Hero's guilt much more weighty than it is in Bandello's tale; here he borrows from Ariosto's version the idea of the maid (Margaret) disguised to look like her mistress, and also the faithful friend who acts as corroborating witness (in Ariosto's story, Lurcanio, Ariodante's brother; in the play, Don Pedro). Indeed, Shakespeare goes further than Ariosto in elaborating the signs of Hero's guilt; not only are we told that Margaret shows herself at the window, dressed in Hero's clothes, to Claudio and Don Pedro, but, in addition, Borachio says that he has wooed Margaret by the name of Hero, so that Claudio and Don Pedro have the testimony of ears as well as eyes on which to base their accusations against Hero. The effect of this is to remove all censure for his rejection of Hero from Claudio, since the proofs are strong against her, and are guaranteed by that soul of honour, the Prince himself, Don Pedro of Aragon, as well as by the confession of Borachio:

> *Upon mine honour,*
> *Myself, my brother, and this grievèd Count*
> *Did see her, hear her, at that hour last night*
> *Talk with a ruffian at her chamber-window;*
> *Who hath, indeed, most like a liberal villain,*
> *Confessed the vile encounters they have had*
> *A thousand times in secret.* IV.1.86–92

Claudio is sometimes attacked as being prim and shallow, but perhaps Shakespeare's point in establishing his good faith, and a substantial appearance of guilt in Hero, was precisely to display Claudio as a most conventional young man, who loves by the rules, woos through intermediaries, and seems as much concerned about Leonato's wealth as he is about Leonato's daughter. He is a romantic lover for whom ardour is unnecessary, since he loves an image rather than a person, and is never seen making love to Hero. Her name signified devotion in love, as the legendary Hero, a priestess of Venus, loved Leander (see V.2.30), who swam the Hellespont nightly to visit her, a story celebrated in Christopher Marlowe's famous poem *Hero and Leander*, completed by George Chapman, and published in 1598, not long before *Much Ado About Nothing* was written. Claudio takes her for granted, and his passion in anger when he learns of her apparent infidelity exceeds all the passion he has ever shown in love. He focuses his rejection of her on her name, asking of her only one question:

> *Let me but move one question to your daughter;*
> *And, by that fatherly and kindly power*
> *That you have in her, bid her answer truly.*

LEONATO
I charge thee do so, as thou art my child.

16

HERO

>*O God defend me! How am I beset!*
>*What kind of catechizing call you this?*

CLAUDIO

>*To make you answer truly to your name.*

HERO

>*Is it not Hero? Who can blot that name*
>*With any just reproach?*

CLAUDIO   *Marry, that can Hero;*
>*Hero itself can blot out Hero's virtue.*   IV.1.71–80

The name by which Claudio had set such store as an emblem of chaste love has become transformed, for he has discovered that Hero's appearance, her name, does not correspond to his idea of virtue in her, and he is lost in paradoxes about her as 'most foul, most fair' (IV.1.101).

Shakespeare invented Don John, whose villainous scheming brings Hero and Claudio to this point. In the story as told by Bandello and Ariosto, jealousy on the part of a rival lover prompts the deception practised on the hero, and, in the one, the reconciliation of friends, in the other, revenge upon a lustful duke, is necessary to complete the tale. Don John, however, has no personal interest in Claudio or Hero; he is a professed enemy of good, a 'plain-dealing villain', who has an abstract love of mischief. He needs no motive, even though he finds one in that Claudio overcame him in battle (I.3.61–2), for he is framed of treachery, and bears all the world a grudge. In the otherwise festive society of Messina, he stands in solitary discontent, and, with his henchmen Conrade and Borachio, embodies sketchily, though not negligibly, the force of evil and destruction in humanity. Don John's independence as a villain relieves Claudio of any responsibility for punishing him, for he is everyone's enemy, and offends society as a whole. The emphasis in the presentation of Claudio is, then, on his sense of honour and conformity to the codes prescribed by convention: he loves Hero as a name rather than as a person, and is perhaps fortunate in the end to find that after all Hero lives up to the chastity implied in her name.

*

Don John's evil produces good in the end, for it provokes the crisis of the play, and results in a strengthening of love. In terms of action on the stage, this is splendidly contrived in the public repudiation by Claudio of Hero in the church. Some have wondered why Shakespeare does not show Borachio at Hero's window, with Don Pedro and Claudio watching him, and indeed this could have made a fine scene; but the dramatic emphasis had to fall on the scene in church (IV.1), for what happens here is the climax of the play's development. In rejecting Hero publicly, Claudio is not being peculiarly nasty, but acts in character; his wooing has been formal and public, he shames Hero in public, and does public penance when he learns of her innocence. For in V.3 he does not go alone to 'Hang her an epitaph upon her tomb', but accompanied by Don Pedro and a group of attendants. He lives, so to speak, in public, in society; privacy is for Benedick and Beatrice, who are left on stage after Hero has been carried off, to bring the scene to a personal focus.

After the theatrical excitements of the church scene, with the rejected Hero swooning, her father Leonato crying out in anguish, and the convenient intervention of Friar Francis with his plot for allowing Hero to be given out as dead, the prose conversation of Benedick and Beatrice might seem a quiet ending to the scene; but it is only in the intimacy of prose that they speak directly to each other, and simultaneously at this point confess their love, and put it to the test.

It is a brilliant dramatic stroke, to make the softening of
mood consequent on the suffering of Hero work on Benedick and Beatrice and bring them to confess:

BENEDICK *I do love nothing in the world so well as you; is
not that strange?*
BEATRICE *As strange as the thing I know not. It were as
possible for me to say I loved nothing so well as you. . . .*
                                                    IV.1.264–7

This is a critical point in the action also because Hero,
Beatrice's close friend, has suffered calumny, and the
declaration of love leads inevitably to the culmination of
this whole scene, not in histrionics, but in Beatrice's quiet
demand of a lover who offers to do anything for her: 'Kill
Claudio' (IV.1.285).

Here, for a moment, it seems almost possible that Don
John's villainy might stir Benedick to revenge, and so lead
to further enmity and bloodshed; for a moment we, the
audience, are exposed to the idea of a growth and spread of
evil, and from this stems the power of Beatrice's words.
For here, in the shadow of the rejection of Hero, Benedick
and Beatrice shed briefly their armour of wit, and speak
plainly and directly, so that we are made to sense the
seriousness of the occasion. Moreover, Beatrice's demand,
'Kill Claudio', is not merely a cry from the heart for
revenge on the man who has brutally harmed her friend;
it is also an immediate and extreme test of the quality of
that love Benedick has just declared for her, requiring him
to put his love for her above his friendship with Claudio.
Benedick goes off to issue his challenge, but the exposure
of Don John's treachery is already in hand, and the duel
does not take place. Don John's villainy does, indeed, provide appropriate ways of putting the love of Claudio and

19

Benedick to the test. Claudio's love, the public avowal of appropriate feelings for a wealthy man's daughter, coloured with romantic terms, is tested in his behaviour when he thinks Hero dead; he fulfils the required public repentance and accepts the wife Leonato offers him, and so shows that he will be a dutiful and honourable husband. Benedick's affection, a more powerful and personal devotion to Beatrice for her own sake, is put to the proof when he is invited to kill Claudio, and it is revealed as love indeed.

This is a major theme of the play, and both pairs of lovers end well-matched; the action has put them to the test, and they earn their success in love. Some feel that Claudio gets more and better than he deserves, but Hero belongs to the same convention, and plays the game by the same rules as he. These superficially romantic lovers live in a world of appearances and proprieties which are more important than personal relationships; Benedick and Beatrice are the true romantics, concealing their passion under a cool flow of wit. At the end, all is harmony: Leonato is pleased to have Hero restored to Claudio; Don Pedro's honour is satisfied; Don John is taken prisoner; and the couples are well matched. Appropriately Benedick calls for a dance, the fitting emblem of concord; for the order and design of the dance suggested very powerfully to the Elizabethan mind an idea of heavenly harmony, of an ordered world, and a society of men living in perfect agreement and proportion. So Sir John Davies wrote in his *Orchestra* (1596):

> Lo! this is Dancing's true nobility,
> Dancing, the child of Music and of love;
> Dancing itself, both love and harmony,
> Where all agree and all in order move;
> Dancing, the art that all arts do approve;

The fair character of the world's consent,
The heaven's true figure, and the earth's ornament.

*

Dogberry, Verges, and the Watchmen do not appear in the final scene, which, with its masked ladies, restores the elegance and style of the earlier dance in II.1, and completes the pattern initiated by the opening scenes of the play. Nevertheless, they serve an important function. They first appear rather late in the action, in III.3, at the point where Don John's plot against Hero seems about to come to fruition. At once their incompetence is established, with Dogberry's instructions to the Watch to avoid all trouble: 'The most peaceable way for you, if you do take a thief, is to let him show himself what he is and steal out of your company' (III.3.56–8). In a world where the officers of the law are so inefficient, no serious villainy can be expected to take place, or a better policing would have been established. So Dogberry and Verges are reassuing figures, and their comic ineptitude establishes a perspective in which we know instinctively that Don John cannot succeed in his mischief, and this is confirmed when later in the scene Borachio and Conrade fall foul of the Watch, and are arrested.

Dogberry and Verges set each other off; Verges is to be imagined as elderly and small, Dogberry as a little younger and much larger (see III.5.32–9) – a Laurel and Hardy pair, in which Verges continually serves as a foil to the complacency and verbosity of his partner. Dogberry insists on taking precedence in all things, even to the extent of being written down an ass, and his role has always been a major one for actors since William Kemp, the famous clown of Shakespeare's company, played the part. What gives him prominence is his abounding vitality. In this he compares, as some subtler interpreters of *Much Ado About Nothing* have noted, with Benedick and Beatrice. Like them he has a commanding energy which finds its outlet in an obsession with words; and like them he has a fine confidence in his own cleverness. The difference, indeed, lies in the obtuseness which his parade of self-assurance in fact reveals; in garbling words, and making rich nonsense, he can be seen as providing a parody of the wordplay of Benedick and Beatrice. His complacent trust in his knowledge and abilities is a comic form of vainglory or *hubris*, which reaches its nadir in his arrogant and self-centred treatment of Verges before Leonato:

> *A good old man, sir, he will be talking; as they say, 'When the age is in, the wit is out.' God help us, it is a world to see! Well said, i'faith, neighbour Verges; well, God's a good man; an two men ride of a horse, one must ride behind. An honest soul, i'faith, sir, by my troth he is, as ever broke bread. But God is to be worshipped; all men are not alike. Alas, good neighbour!* III.5.32–8

Such patronizing is unbearable, and it has been well noted that if Dogberry were a real official he would be insufferable. It is, then, a splendidly fitting culmination of his role that he should, in a last excess of self-importance, insist on having Conrade's dismissal of him as an ass remembered and recorded: 'But, masters, remember that I am an ass; though it be not written down, yet forget not that I am an ass' (IV.2.74–6). So in the end he exposes and brands himself.

At the same time, Dogberry, Verges, and the Watchmen bring a human warmth into the somewhat rarefied atmosphere of courtly Messina, and a sense of the common touch. They round out the world of the play, and provide a bridge between remote Sicily and an English audience. Dogberry tells his deputy, 'you, constable, are to present the Prince's own person' (III.3.72–3); in thus representing the Prince, he embodies a distant and awe-inspiring authority in a common and familiar figure. In Dogberry also the petty tyranny of the small official is made ridiculous, and therefore tolerable. His triumph is to be asked by Leonato to examine Borachio and Conrade. Leonato, by a fine stroke of irony, is hurrying to church to give Hero in marriage, and cannot stay to examine the malefactors, and so learn of the villainy being practised against his daughter. So Dogberry takes over the magistrate's role, and sits gowned in full state to interrogate the prisoners. The *petit bourgeois* clown 'that hath two gowns and everything handsome about him' (IV.2.82–3) acts in the place of the nobleman or prince, and so brings the role of prince down to earth, parodying, and so mocking, the trappings and exercise of power.

*

The panoply of this interrogation is related to other ceremonial occasions in the play. The action has seemed to some a game, in which dances and garden-scenes, eavesdropping, mistakes, and disguises establish a playful pattern, and compose a light comedy of errors. However, Shakespeare skilfully breaks the tone and movement of the action with the solemn ritual of the wedding in church in IV.1. On the stage, the visual effect of this scene is most important. The stage in Shakespeare's own theatre had little scope for scenery, so far as is known, but all kinds of properties and effects could be contrived. The façade at the rear of the stage looked rather like an elaborate interior of a large house, with its doors and gallery, but could serve equally well to suggest the exterior of a house, with the stage as street, court, or garden. No doubt for the garden scenes in *Much Ado About Nothing* property trees, and an arbour, were brought on stage. The church scene required much more, perhaps a processional entry, with priests or assistants robed and bearing candles or censers, and other suggestions of a church. Very probably the family monument of Leonato, mentioned at IV.1.204, is present on stage, and adds to the effect of this scene. It is seen again in V.3, when Claudio comes ceremonially to mourn over the Hero he thinks is dead, and to have a dirge sung for her. The solemnity, and sense of ritual, in the scenes lend them dignity and provide a marked change of atmosphere from the earlier gaiety.

It is true that the appearance from time to time of Dogberry and Verges keeps the comic purpose of the play in mind. It is also true that the audience know of Don John's plot, and are aware that Claudio is deceived in respect both of Hero's supposed infidelity, and her supposed death. In addition, Shakespeare gives the two old men, Leonato, and his brother Antonio, a mildly comic scene in V.1, in which Antonio begins by preaching patience to the distraught Leonato (who is passionate in anger against Claudio) and ends by becoming even more angry than Leonato. In spite of this necessary maintenance of the comic tone, the seriousness and solemnity introduced with the ritual of the church scene modify the play's atmosphere sufficiently to make temporarily vivid the reality of pain and evil, and to give a splendid dramatic force to Beatrice's injunction to Benedick, 'Kill Claudio'. The last scene of the play then brings back with renewed vigour the full sunshine and high spirits of the opening, but enhanced by the promise of marriage and felicity for all except Don John. This play, in which music and dance are prominent, may justly be compared to a symphony which, beginning animatedly in a major key, drops into a minor key, clouded for a time with discords and anguish, only to finish in the gayest *allegro vivace*.

*

The greater part of *Much Ado About Nothing* is written in prose, and the characters whose speech is almost wholly in prose (Beatrice and Benedick; Dogberry and Verges) have more life and depth than those who speak verse most of the time (Claudio, Leonato, Antonio, Hero). In this play such a contrast seems natural, for like Berowne in *Love's Labour's Lost* (V.2.406–7), Benedick and Beatrice deliberately reject

> *Taffeta phrases, silken terms precise,*
> *Three-piled hyperboles, spruce affectation,*

in favour of witty prose; and Claudio and Hero, with their rather artificial verse, seem intended to expose in some measure the emptiness of romantic poses in love. The influence has been noted here of the witty prose comedies of John Lyly, written in the 1580s for boys to act. The style of the opening scene of *Much Ado About Nothing* has some echoes of the antithetical and alliterative style popularized by Lyly in his novel *Euphues, the Anatomy of Wit* (1578, and often reprinted), and employed by him more subtly in his dramatic dialogue:

> *doing, in the figure of a lamb, the feats of a lion.* . . .
> *Much Ado About Nothing*, I.1.14–15

> *I choose rather to pine in this castle, than to be a prince in*
> *any other court.*   Lyly, *Endymion*, III.2.14–15

Such patternings suggest a consciousness on Shakespeare's part of the techniques of Lyly, and he makes use of them even while gently mocking them.

However, there may have been more compelling reasons for Shakespeare's devotion to prose in *Much Ado About Nothing*. At the stage of his career when he wrote this play, he seems to have been working through a transition period in his handling of blank verse, as though the verse medium

25

in which he had created successfully a range of characters in his earlier plays, notably *Richard III* and *Richard II*, was no longer proving suitable, or flexible enough, for a more mature dramatic art. For a few years he wrote plays in which major characters speak chiefly in prose (like Falstaff, Rosalind in *As You Like It*, and Benedick and Beatrice) or which contain a great deal of dialogue in prose (like *Henry V*, and *Twelfth Night*). Had there been no other evidence for dating *Much Ado About Nothing*, the superiority of the 'prose' to the 'verse' characters would have been enough to suggest a placing in this group.

In fact, the date of the play can be determined between reasonably narrow limits. It is not mentioned in the famous list of Shakespeare's 'excellent' comedies in *Palladis Tamia: Wit's Treasury*, by Francis Meres, printed late in 1598; and William Kemp, the clown who is named for the part of Dogberry in speech-prefixes in IV.2, left Shakespeare's company of actors, the Lord Chamberlain's Men, early in 1599. Richard Cowley, another actor in this company, is named for Verges also in the Quarto, showing that Shakespeare thought of some of his characters, at any rate, in terms of the actors he worked with. Another actor, or rather musician, 'Jacke Wilson', is named in the Folio text at II.3.34, where the Quarto merely calls for music; but little more is known of this John Wilson than that at some time before 1623 he sang 'Sigh no more, ladies' in a production of *Much Ado About Nothing*.

The play has a few problems for the producer. Shakespeare's stage, a platform extending into an arena surrounded by galleries of spectators, offered to the audience a large acting-area in front of a permanent façade; different parts of this main acting-area could readily have served for the main action of *Much Ado About Nothing*, which is located in Leonato's house, or in a street, court or garden nearby. The garden or orchard, with its 'arbour' (II.3.34) where first Benedick, and later on Beatrice, overhear what others say of them, may have been suggested by a few properties. It is probable that the scene in church (IV.1), and the scene where Claudio mourns at the family tomb of Leonato (V.3), were made impressive by costume, ceremonial processions, and a few ecclesiastical properties. On the modern stage, these scenes offer great scope for invention, and much ingenuity has been exercised on transforming the stage to suggest a church. The 'Kill Claudio' sequence of dialogue between Beatrice and Benedick was expanded and transformed into a climax of confrontation by J. P. Kemble in a version of the play that held the stage through the nineteenth century, and a true sense of the quiet power of this scene has been recovered only recently, notably through the performance of John Gielgud as Benedick, beginning in 1950 (see J. F. Cox's article in *Shakespeare Survey* 32, 1979). To establish here the right tone, and achieve the necessary solemnity without losing the style and grace of earlier scenes, is perhaps the hardest task for the producer. Yet this is not to be thought of as a major difficulty; for the play has such an abundance of vitality, music, and wit that it will surely continue to challenge and attract producer, actor, and audience alike.

FURTHER READING

While not denying that the play is a romantic comedy, the three major twentieth-century editions of *Much Ado* – A. R. Humphreys's Arden (1981), F. H. Mares's New Cambridge (1988) and Sheldon Zitner's Oxford (1993) – seem most eager to deal with the play in terms of its affinities with the problem plays and Romances rather than with *As You Like It* and *Twelfth Night*. Zitner's *Much Ado*, for instance, resonates with 'the problematic realism of *The Taming of the Shrew*, *All's Well* and *Measure for Measure*'. This approach has attracted a number of critics: Carol T. Neely's book *Broken Nuptials in Shakespeare's Plays* (1985) discusses *Much Ado* with *All's Well*, *Antony and Cleopatra*, *Othello* and *The Winter's Tale*; A. P. Rossiter's *Angel with Horns* (1961), which talks of *Much Ado*'s wit and its theme of imperfect self-knowledge, treats the play in the company of essays on the Second Part of *Henry IV*, *Troilus and Cressida*, *All's Well*, *Othello*, *Hamlet* and *Measure for Measure*; and Joseph Westlund's *Shakespeare's Reparative Comedies: A Psychoanalytic View of the Middle Plays* (1984), which brackets all three romantic comedies with *The Merchant of Venice*, *All's Well* and *Measure for Measure*, places *Much Ado* in a therapeutic discussion of 'how these plays help to repair our inner worlds'. Despite these 'adult' affinities, there is, as Mares points out, less criticism of *Much Ado* than of the other romantic comedies, though the play has always been a favourite in the theatre.

Zitner focusses on the play's 'broad sunless patches'. There is, he notes, nothing supernatural at work in *Much Ado*; nothing pastoral; no fairy-tale. What we have, by and large, is sophisticated, rather cruel 'drawing-room banter'. Of the oft-noted discrepancy between the two pairs of lovers, he sensibly suggests that Elizabethan audiences would simply see the Hero–Claudio plot as working in a different, more literary, convention; for them the relationship between Beatrice and Benedick would be more humanly recognizable, as it is for us. He notes how difficult it is in the theatre to get a balanced partnership between Benedick and Beatrice – one of the most successful was Judi Dench and Donald Sinden in Stratford in 1976. Zitner is equally common-sensical about the modernity of Beatrice: 'Though something of the feminist that Ellen Terry . . . praised her for being, Beatrice is of her class and day. Occasionally her statements have connotations that time has made more radical than the character'. Such a hard-headed view is supported – trenchantly – by Marilyn Williamson's feminist *The Patriarchy of Shakespeare's Comedies* (1986) when she argues that 'The fact that the most attractive representations of women – those in the romantic comedies and the romances – are part of fantasies which extend male profit and power is a disturbing thought'. For her, Shakespeare's plays 'seem protofeminist and yet [are] patriarchal to the core'.

The social dimensions of the play have been taken up most recently by Camille Slights in her book *Shakespeare's Comic Commonwealths* (1993). Richard A. Levin's *Love and Society in Shakesperean Comedy* (1985) has a good analysis of Messina's shortcomings. Leonard Tennenhouse in *Power on Display: The Politics of Shakespeare's Genres* (1986) sees *Much Ado* as part of a mockery of aristocratic culture 'which sharply distinguished Elizabethan romantic comedy both from preceding comic forms and from the Jacobean city comedy'. Penny Gay's subversive feminist history of Shakespeare's comedies in the theatre, *As She Likes It: Shakespeare's Unruly Women* (1994), deals with productions of *Much Ado* from 1949 to 1990.

Not all recent sophisticated criticism eschews J. Dover Wilson's thesis in *Shakespeare's Happy Comedies* (1962), though it would be hard to find an endorsement for his inclusion of Claudio in our happy feelings about the play. What we do find are variations of Kiernan Ryan's shaky argument in *Shakespeare* (1989) that the comedies were intended by Shakespeare to be in vivid, heuristic contrast to real Elizabethan life: the titles of the romantic comedies alert us to 'a privileged realm beyond the reach of the authorities that ordinarily programme and discipline people's lives'. R. C.

Hassel's biblically minded *Faith and Folly in Shakespeare's Romantic Comedies* (1980) emphasizes the educative value of the games the lovers play in the comedies. E. J. Jensen's *Shakespeare and the Ends of Comedy* (1991) urges us to value these games without bothering too much about how the plays end (he admits that they end with a return to the patriarchal status quo), despite the arguments to the contrary by a host of critics, including C. L. Barber and Northrop Frye. This is especially the case with *Much Ado*: 'Of all Shakespeare's comedies, *Much Ado About Nothing* seems most uncongenial to interpretations that look for meaning to emerge at the point of closure'. Hassel urges us to abandon our traditional concern for 'teleological design' – there is no isolable truth, he says, enacted in the final scene. So much for male profit and power.

Useful introductory studies of *Much Ado* include: J. R. Mulryne's *'Much Ado About Nothing'* (1965), Walter R. Davis's compilation of *Twentieth Century Interpretations* of the play (1969), Ralph Berry's *Shakespeare's Comedies: Explorations in Form* (1972), Kenneth Muir's *Shakespeare's Comic Sequence* (1979), Bertrand Evans's *Shakespeare's Comedies* (1960), Leo Salingar's *Shakespeare and the Traditions of Comedy* (1974), Peter G. Phialas's *Shakespeare's Romantic Comedies: The Development of their Form and Meaning* (1966) (self-confessedly introductory) and David Richman's *Laughter, Pain, and Wonder: Shakespeare's Comedies and the Audience in the Theater* (1990). Alexander Leggatt's *Shakespeare's Comedy of Love* (1974) is valuable for its thoughtful analysis of the *differences* between the romantic comedies – compare Berry; John Russell Brown's selection of essays on *Much Ado* and *As You Like It* in the Casebook Series (1979) is to be commended for its section on the comedies on the stage (1888–1967) and for reprinting Sherman Hawkins's invaluable essay 'The Two Worlds of Shakespearean Comedy'. An equally valuable essay of more recent vintage is Harold Jenkins's 'The Ball-Scene in *Much Ado About Nothing*' in *Shakespeare: Text, Language, Criticism* (1987) edited by B. Fabian and K. T. von Rosador. Richard Levin's *The Multiple Plot in English Renaissance Drama* (1971) has a detailed and fascinating analysis of the formal connections between the two plots of *Much Ado*. And Charles T. Prouty's *The Sources of 'Much Ado About Nothing'* (1950) tells us a good deal about Shakespeare's use of his sources, though it does seem excessive to have half the book taken up with a reprint of one of them, the verse narrative *The Historie of Ariodonto and Ienura* (1565–6) by Peter Beverley.

Michael Taylor, 1996

MUCH ADO ABOUT NOTHING

THE CHARACTERS IN THE PLAY

DON PEDRO, Prince of Arragon
BENEDICK, of Padua ⎱ young lords, companions of Don
CLAUDIO, of Florence ⎰ Pedro
DON JOHN, Don Pedro's bastard brother
BORACHIO ⎱
CONRADE ⎰ followers of Don John
LEONATO, Governor of Messina
ANTONIO, his brother, an old man
BALTHASAR, a singer
FRIAR FRANCIS, a priest

HERO, Leonato's daughter
MARGARET ⎱
URSULA ⎰ attendants on Hero
BEATRICE, an orphan, Leonato's niece

DOGBERRY, the Constable in charge of the Watch
VERGES, the Headborough, Dogberry's partner in authority
A Sexton, and several Watchmen, under Dogberry's
authority

A Boy, servant to Benedick
Attendants and musicians in Leonato's household
Messengers

*Enter Leonato, Governor of Messina, Hero, his
daughter, Beatrice, his niece, with a Messenger*

LEONATO I learn in this letter that Don Pedro of Arragon
comes this night to Messina.

MESSENGER He is very near by this; he was not three
leagues off when I left him.

LEONATO How many gentlemen have you lost in this
action?

MESSENGER But few of any sort, and none of name.

LEONATO A victory is twice itself when the achiever brings
home full numbers. I find here that Don Pedro hath
bestowed much honour on a young Florentine called 10
Claudio.

MESSENGER Much deserved on his part and equally remembered by Don Pedro. He hath borne himself beyond the promise of his age, doing, in the figure of a
lamb, the feats of a lion; he hath indeed better bettered
expectation than you must expect of me to tell you how.

LEONATO He hath an uncle here in Messina will be very
much glad of it.

MESSENGER I have already delivered him letters, and
there appears much joy in him; even so much that joy 20
could not show itself modest enough without a badge of
bitterness.

LEONATO Did he break out into tears?

MESSENGER In great measure.

LEONATO A kind overflow of kindness; there are no faces
truer than those that are so washed. How much better is
it to weep at joy than to joy at weeping!

37

BEATRICE I pray you, is Signor Mountanto returned from the wars, or no?

30 MESSENGER I know none of that name, lady; there was none such in the army of any sort.

LEONATO What is he that you ask for, niece?

HERO My cousin means Signor Benedick of Padua.

MESSENGER O, he's returned, and as pleasant as ever he was.

BEATRICE He set up his bills here in Messina, and challenged Cupid at the flight; and my uncle's fool, reading the challenge, subscribed for Cupid, and challenged him at the bird-bolt. I pray you, how many hath he killed and

40 eaten in these wars? But how many hath he killed? For indeed, I promised to eat all of his killing.

LEONATO Faith, niece, you tax Signor Benedick too much; but he'll be meet with you, I doubt it not.

MESSENGER He hath done good service, lady, in these wars.

BEATRICE You had musty victual, and he hath holp to eat it; he is a very valiant trencher-man, he hath an excellent stomach.

MESSENGER And a good soldier too, lady.

50 BEATRICE And a good soldier to a lady. But what is he to a lord?

MESSENGER A lord to a lord, a man to a man, stuffed with all honourable virtues.

BEATRICE It is so, indeed; he is no less than a stuffed man; but for the stuffing – well, we are all mortal.

LEONATO You must not, sir, mistake my niece. There is a kind of merry war betwixt Signor Benedick and her; they never meet but there's a skirmish of wit between them.

60 BEATRICE Alas, he gets nothing by that. In our last conflict four of his five wits went halting off, and now is the

38

whole man governed with one; so that if he have wit enough to keep himself warm, let him bear it for a difference between himself and his horse; for it is all the wealth that he hath left, to be known a reasonable creature. Who is his companion now? He hath every month a new sworn brother.

MESSENGER Is't possible?

BEATRICE Very easily possible: he wears his faith but as the fashion of his hat; it ever changes with the next 70 block.

MESSENGER I see, lady, the gentleman is not in your books.

BEATRICE No; an he were, I would burn my study. But, I pray you, who is his companion? Is there no young squarer now that will make a voyage with him to the devil?

MESSENGER He is most in the company of the right noble Claudio.

BEATRICE O Lord, he will hang upon him like a disease. He is sooner caught than the pestilence, and the taker 80 runs presently mad. God help the noble Claudio! If he have caught the Benedick, it will cost him a thousand pound ere 'a be cured.

MESSENGER I will hold friends with you, lady.

BEATRICE Do, good friend.

LEONATO You will never run mad, niece.

BEATRICE No, not till a hot January.

MESSENGER Don Pedro is approached.

Enter Don Pedro, Claudio, Benedick, Balthasar, and Don John the Bastard

DON PEDRO Good Signor Leonato, are you come to meet your trouble? The fashion of the world is to avoid cost, 90 and you encounter it.

LEONATO Never came trouble to my house in the likeness of your grace; for trouble being gone, comfort should remain; but when you depart from me sorrow abides, and happiness takes his leave.

DON PEDRO You embrace your charge too willingly. I think this is your daughter.

LEONATO Her mother hath many times told me so.

BENEDICK Were you in doubt, sir, that you asked her?

100 LEONATO Signor Benedick, no; for then were you a child.

DON PEDRO You have it full, Benedick; we may guess by this what you are, being a man. Truly, the lady fathers herself. Be happy, lady; for you are like an honourable father.

BENEDICK If Signor Leonato be her father, she would not have his head on her shoulders for all Messina, as like him as she is.

BEATRICE I wonder that you will still be talking, Signor Benedick; nobody marks you.

110 BENEDICK What, my dear Lady Disdain! Are you yet living?

BEATRICE Is it possible disdain should die while she hath such meet food to feed it as Signor Benedick? Courtesy itself must convert to disdain, if you come in her presence.

BENEDICK Then is courtesy a turncoat. But it is certain I am loved of all ladies, only you excepted; and I would I could find in my heart that I had not a hard heart, for, truly, I love none.

120 BEATRICE A dear happiness to women; they would else have been troubled with a pernicious suitor! I thank God and my cold blood, I am of your humour for that; I had rather hear my dog bark at a crow than a man swear he loves me.

BENEDICK God keep your ladyship still in that mind! So some gentleman or other shall 'scape a predestinate scratched face.

40

BEATRICE Scratching could not make it worse, an 'twere such a face as yours were.

BENEDICK Well, you are a rare parrot-teacher. 130

BEATRICE A bird of my tongue is better than a beast of yours.

BENEDICK I would my horse had the speed of your tongue, and so good a continuer. But keep your way a' God's name, I have done.

BEATRICE You always end with a jade's trick; I know you of old.

DON PEDRO That is the sum of all, Leonato. Signor Claudio and Signor Benedick, my dear friend Leonato hath invited you all. I tell him we shall stay here at the 140 least a month, and he heartily prays some occasion may detain us longer. I dare swear he is no hypocrite, but prays from his heart.

LEONATO If you swear, my lord, you shall not be for-sworn. (*To Don John*) Let me bid you welcome, my lord, being reconciled to the Prince your brother. I owe you all duty.

DON JOHN I thank you. I am not of many words, but I thank you.

LEONATO Please it your grace lead on? 150

DON PEDRO Your hand, Leonato; we will go together.

Exeunt all except Benedick and Claudio

CLAUDIO Benedick, didst thou note the daughter of Signor Leonato?

BENEDICK I noted her not, but I looked on her.

CLAUDIO Is she not a modest young lady?

BENEDICK Do you question me as an honest man should do, for my simple true judgement? Or would you have me speak after my custom, as being a professed tyrant to their sex?

CLAUDIO No, I pray thee speak in sober judgement. 160

41

BENEDICK Why, i'faith, methinks she's too low for a high praise, too brown for a fair praise, and too little for a great praise; only this commendation I can afford her, that were she other than she is, she were unhandsome; and being no other but as she is, I do not like her.

CLAUDIO Thou thinkest I am in sport; I pray thee tell me truly how thou likest her.

BENEDICK Would you buy her, that you inquire after her?

CLAUDIO Can the world buy such a jewel?

170 BENEDICK Yea, and a case to put it into. But speak you this with a sad brow? Or do you play the flouting Jack, to tell us Cupid is a good hare-finder, and Vulcan a rare carpenter? Come, in what key shall a man take you to go in the song?

CLAUDIO In mine eye she is the sweetest lady that ever I looked on.

BENEDICK I can see yet without spectacles, and I see no such matter; there's her cousin, an she were not possessed with a fury, exceeds her as much in beauty as the

180 first of May doth the last of December. But I hope you have no intent to turn husband, have you?

CLAUDIO I would scarce trust myself, though I had sworn the contrary, if Hero would be my wife.

BENEDICK Is't come to this? In faith, hath not the world one man but he will wear his cap with suspicion? Shall I never see a bachelor of threescore again? Go to, i'faith; an thou wilt needs thrust thy neck into a yoke, wear the print of it, and sigh away Sundays. Look, Don Pedro is returned to seek you.

Enter Don Pedro

190 DON PEDRO What secret hath held you here, that you followed not to Leonato's?

BENEDICK I would your grace would constrain me to tell.

DON PEDRO I charge thee on thy allegiance.

BENEDICK You hear, Count Claudio; I can be secret as a
dumb man, I would have you think so; but, on my allegiance, mark you this, on my allegiance – he is in love.
With who? Now that is your grace's part. Mark how short
his answer is: With Hero, Leonato's short daughter.

CLAUDIO If this were so, so were it uttered.

BENEDICK Like the old tale, my lord: 'It is not so, nor 200
'twas not so; but, indeed, God forbid it should be so!'

CLAUDIO If my passion change not shortly, God forbid it
should be otherwise!

DON PEDRO Amen, if you love her; for the lady is very
well worthy.

CLAUDIO You speak this to fetch me in, my lord.

DON PEDRO By my troth, I speak my thought.

CLAUDIO And in faith, my lord, I spoke mine.

BENEDICK And by my two faiths and troths, my lord, I
spoke mine. 210

CLAUDIO That I love her, I feel.

DON PEDRO That she is worthy, I know.

BENEDICK That I neither feel how she should be loved,
nor know how she should be worthy, is the opinion that
fire cannot melt out of me; I will die in it at the stake.

DON PEDRO Thou wast ever an obstinate heretic in the
despite of beauty.

CLAUDIO And never could maintain his part but in the
force of his will.

BENEDICK That a woman conceived me, I thank her; that 220
she brought me up, I likewise give her most humble
thanks; but that I will have a recheat winded in my
forehead, or hang my bugle in an invisible baldrick, all
women shall pardon me. Because I will not do them the
wrong to mistrust any, I will do myself the right to trust
none; and the fine is, for the which I may go the finer, I
will live a bachelor.

DON PEDRO I shall see thee, ere I die, look pale with love.

BENEDICK With anger, with sickness, or with hunger, my
230   lord, not with love. Prove that ever I lose more blood
with love than I will get again with drinking, pick out
mine eyes with a ballad-maker's pen and hang me up
at the door of a brothel-house for the sign of blind
Cupid.

DON PEDRO Well, if ever thou dost fall from this faith,
thou wilt prove a notable argument.

BENEDICK If I do, hang me in a bottle like a cat, and shoot
at me; and he that hits me, let him be clapped on the
shoulder, and called Adam.

240 DON PEDRO Well, as time shall try:
'In time the savage bull doth bear the yoke.'

BENEDICK The savage bull may; but if ever the sensible
Benedick bear it, pluck off the bull's horns and set them
in my forehead, and let me be vilely painted; and in such
great letters as they write 'Here is good horse to hire',
let them signify under my sign 'Here you may see
Benedick the married man.'

CLAUDIO If this should ever happen, thou wouldst be
horn-mad.

250 DON PEDRO Nay, if Cupid have not spent all his quiver in
Venice, thou wilt quake for this shortly.

BENEDICK I look for an earthquake too, then.

DON PEDRO Well, you will temporize with the hours. In
the meantime, good Signor Benedick, repair to Leonato's, commend me to him and tell him I will not fail
him at supper; for indeed he hath made great preparation.

BENEDICK I have almost matter enough in me for such an
embassage; and so I commit you –

260 CLAUDIO To the tuition of God. From my house, if I had
it –

44

DON PEDRO The sixth of July. Your loving friend, Benedick.

BENEDICK Nay, mock not, mock not. The body of your discourse is sometime guarded with fragments, and the guards are but slightly basted on neither. Ere you flout old ends any further, examine your conscience; and so I leave you. *Exit*

CLAUDIO
My liege, your highness now may do me good.

DON PEDRO
My love is thine to teach; teach it but how, 270
And thou shalt see how apt it is to learn
Any hard lesson that may do thee good.

CLAUDIO
Hath Leonato any son, my lord?

DON PEDRO
No child but Hero; she's his only heir.
Dost thou affect her, Claudio?

CLAUDIO   O, my lord,
When you went onward on this ended action,
I looked upon her with a soldier's eye,
That liked, but had a rougher task in hand
Than to drive liking to the name of love;
But now I am returned and that war-thoughts 280
Have left their places vacant, in their rooms
Come thronging soft and delicate desires,
All prompting me how fair young Hero is,
Saying I liked her ere I went to wars.

DON PEDRO
Thou wilt be like a lover presently
And tire the hearer with a book of words.
If thou dost love fair Hero, cherish it,
And I will break with her and with her father
And thou shalt have her. Was't not to this end

45

290   That thou began'st to twist so fine a story?

CLAUDIO

How sweetly you do minister to love,
That know love's grief by his complexion!
But lest my liking might too sudden seem,
I would have salved it with a longer treatise.

DON PEDRO

What need the bridge much broader than the flood?
The fairest grant is the necessity.
Look what will serve is fit. 'Tis once, thou lovest,
And I will fit thee with the remedy.
I know we shall have revelling tonight;
300   I will assume thy part in some disguise
And tell fair Hero I am Claudio,
And in her bosom I'll unclasp my heart,
And take her hearing prisoner with the force
And strong encounter of my amorous tale.
Then after, to her father will I break,
And the conclusion is, she shall be thine.
In practice let us put it presently.   *Exeunt*

I.2   *Enter Leonato meeting an old man, his brother Antonio*

LEONATO How now, brother! Where is my cousin, your
son? Hath he provided this music?

ANTONIO He is very busy about it. But, brother, I can tell
you strange news that you yet dreamt not of.

LEONATO Are they good?

ANTONIO As the event stamps them; but they have a
good cover, they show well outward. The Prince and
Count Claudio, walking in a thick-pleached alley in
mine orchard, were thus much overheard by a man of
10   mine: the Prince discovered to Claudio that he loved
my niece your daughter, and meant to acknowledge it

46

this night in a dance; and if he found her accordant, he meant to take the present time by the top and instantly break with you of it.

LEONATO Hath the fellow any wit that told you this?

ANTONIO A good sharp fellow; I will send for him, and question him yourself.

LEONATO No, no; we will hold it as a dream, till it appear itself; but I will acquaint my daughter withal, that she be the better prepared for an answer, if peradventure 20 this be true. Go you and tell her of it.

Attendants cross the stage, led by Antonio's son, and accompanied by Balthasar the musician

Cousin, you know what you have to do. (*To the musician*) O, I cry you mercy, friend; go you with me, and I will use your skill. Good cousin, have a care this busy time.

Exeunt

Enter Don John the Bastard and Conrade his   I.3
companion

CONRADE What the good-year, my lord! Why are you thus out of measure sad?

DON JOHN There is no measure in the occasion that breeds; therefore the sadness is without limit.

CONRADE You should hear reason.

DON JOHN And when I have heard it, what blessing brings it?

CONRADE If not a present remedy, at least a patient sufferance.

DON JOHN I wonder that thou – being, as thou sayest thou 10 art, born under Saturn – goest about to apply a moral medicine to a mortifying mischief. I cannot hide what I am. I must be sad when I have cause, and smile at no man's jests; eat when I have stomach, and wait for no

man's leisure; sleep when I am drowsy, and tend on no
man's business; laugh when I am merry, and claw no
man in his humour.

CONRADE Yea, but you must not make the full show of this
till you may do it without controlment. You have of late
20 stood out against your brother, and he hath ta'en you
newly into his grace, where it is impossible you should
take true root but by the fair weather that you make
yourself; it is needful that you frame the season for your
own harvest.

DON JOHN I had rather be a canker in a hedge than a rose
in his grace, and it better fits my blood to be disdained
of all than to fashion a carriage to rob love from any. In
this, though I cannot be said to be a flattering honest
man, it must not be denied but I am a plain-dealing
30 villain. I am trusted with a muzzle and enfranchised with
a clog; therefore I have decreed not to sing in my cage.
If I had my mouth, I would bite; if I had my liberty, I
would do my liking. In the meantime, let me be that I
am, and seek not to alter me.

CONRADE Can you make no use of your discontent?

DON JOHN I make all use of it, for I use it only. Who
comes here?

Enter Borachio

What news, Borachio?

BORACHIO I came yonder from a great supper. The Prince
40 your brother is royally entertained by Leonato; and I can
give you intelligence of an intended marriage.

DON JOHN Will it serve for any model to build mischief
on? What is he for a fool that betroths himself to
unquietness?

BORACHIO Marry, it is your brother's right hand.

DON JOHN Who? The most exquisite Claudio?

BORACHIO Even he.

DON JOHN A proper squire! And who, and who? Which way looks he?

BORACHIO Marry, on Hero, the daughter and heir of 50 Leonato.

DON JOHN A very forward March-chick! How came you to this?

BORACHIO Being entertained for a perfumer, as I was smoking a musty room, comes me the Prince and Claudio, hand in hand, in sad conference. I whipt me behind the arras, and there heard it agreed upon that the Prince should woo Hero for himself, and having obtained her, give her to Count Claudio.

spying (deceit mst)

DON JOHN Come, come, let us thither; this may prove 60 food to my displeasure. That young start-up hath all the glory of my overthrow; if I can cross him any way, I bless myself every way. You are both sure, and will assist me?

CONRADE To the death, my lord.

DON JOHN Let us to the great supper; their cheer is the greater that I am subdued. Would the cook were o'my mind! Shall we go prove what's to be done?

BORACHIO We'll wait upon your lordship.   *Exeunt*

*

Enter Leonato, Antonio, Hero, Beatrice, Margaret,   II.1
and Ursula

LEONATO Was not Count John here at supper?

ANTONIO I saw him not.

BEATRICE How tartly that gentleman looks! I never can see him but I am heart-burned an hour after.

HERO He is of a very melancholy disposition. *(Don John)*

BEATRICE He were an excellent man that were made just

49

in the midway between him and Benedick; the one is too like an image and says nothing, and the other too like my lady's eldest son, evermore tattling.

10 LEONATO Then half Signor Benedick's tongue in Count John's mouth, and half Count John's melancholy in Signor Benedick's face –

BEATRICE With a good leg and a good foot, uncle, and money enough in his purse, such a man would win any woman in the world, if 'a could get her good will.

LEONATO By my troth, niece, thou wilt never get thee a husband if thou be so shrewd of thy tongue.

ANTONIO In faith, she's too curst.

BEATRICE Too curst is more than curst. I shall lessen
20 God's sending that way; for it is said, 'God sends a curst cow short horns', but to a cow too curst he sends none.

LEONATO So, by being too curst, God will send you no horns.

BEATRICE Just, if he send me no husband; for the which blessing I am at him upon my knees every morning and evening. Lord, I could not endure a husband with a beard on his face! I had rather lie in the woollen.

LEONATO You may light on a husband that hath no beard.

BEATRICE What should I do with him? Dress him in my
30 apparel and make him my waiting-gentlewoman? He that hath a beard is more than a youth, and he that hath no beard is less than a man; and he that is more than a youth is not for me, and he that is less than a man, I am not for him. Therefore I will even take sixpence in earnest of the bear-ward, and lead his apes into hell.

LEONATO Well then, go you into hell?

BEATRICE No, but to the gate; and there will the devil meet me, like an old cuckold with horns on his head, and say 'Get you to heaven, Beatrice, get you to heaven;
40 here's no place for you maids.' So deliver I up my apes, and away to Saint Peter for the heavens; he shows me

where the bachelors sit, and there live we as merry as
the day is long.

ANTONIO (*to Hero*) Well, niece, I trust you will be ruled
by your father.

BEATRICE Yes, faith; it is my cousin's duty to make
curtsy and say, 'Father, as it please you'. But yet for all
that, cousin, let him be a handsome fellow, or else make
another curtsy and say, 'Father, as it please me'.

LEONATO Well, niece, I hope to see you one day fitted with 50
a husband.

BEATRICE Not till God make men of some other metal
than earth. Would it not grieve a woman to be over-
mastered with a piece of valiant dust? To make an
account of her life to a clod of wayward marl? No,
uncle, I'll none. Adam's sons are my brethren, and,
truly, I hold it a sin to match in my kindred.

LEONATO Daughter, remember what I told you. If the
Prince do solicit you in that kind, you know your
answer. 60

BEATRICE The fault will be in the music, cousin, if you
be not wooed in good time. If the Prince be too important, tell him there is measure in everything and so dance
out the answer. For hear me, Hero: wooing, wedding,
and repenting, is as a Scotch jig, a measure, and a
cinquepace; the first suit is hot and hasty, like a Scotch
jig, and full as fantastical; the wedding, mannerly-
modest, as a measure, full of state and ancientry; and
then comes repentance and, with his bad legs, falls into
the cinquepace faster and faster, till he sink into his 70
grave.

LEONATO Cousin, you apprehend passing shrewdly.

BEATRICE I have a good eye, uncle; I can see a church
by daylight.

LEONATO The revellers are entering, brother; make good
room.

All put on their masks
Enter Don Pedro, Claudio, Benedick, Balthasar, Don
John, Borachio and others, as masquers, with a drum

DON PEDRO Lady, will you walk a bout with your friend?

HERO So you walk softly, and look sweetly, and say
nothing, I am yours for the walk; and especially when
80 I walk away.

DON PEDRO With me in your company?

HERO I may say so, when I please.

DON PEDRO And when please you to say so?

HERO When I like your favour; for God defend the lute
should be like the case!

DON PEDRO
My visor is Philemon's roof; within the house is Jove.

HERO
Why, then, your visor should be thatched.

DON PEDRO   Speak low, if you speak love.

He draws her aside

BALTHASAR Well, I would you did like me.

MARGARET So would not I, for your own sake; for I have
90 many ill qualities.

BALTHASAR Which is one?

MARGARET I say my prayers aloud.

BALTHASAR I love you the better; the hearers may cry
Amen.

MARGARET God match me with a good dancer!

BALTHASAR Amen.

MARGARET And God keep him out of my sight when the
dance is done! Answer, clerk.

BALTHASAR No more words; the clerk is answered.

100 URSULA I know you well enough; you are Signor Antonio.

ANTONIO At a word, I am not.

URSULA I know you by the waggling of your head.

ANTONIO To tell you true, I counterfeit him.

URSULA You could never do him so ill-well unless you

52

were the very man. Here's his dry hand up and down;
you are he, you are he.

ANTONIO At a word, I am not.

URSULA Come, come, do you think I do not know you by
your excellent wit? Can virtue hide itself? Go to, mum,
you are he; graces will appear, and there's an end.   110

BEATRICE Will you not tell me who told you so?

BENEDICK No, you shall pardon me.

BEATRICE Nor will you not tell me who you are?

BENEDICK Not now.

BEATRICE That I was disdainful, and that I had my good
wit out of the 'Hundred Merry Tales' – well, this was
Signor Benedick that said so.

BENEDICK What's he?

BEATRICE I am sure you know him well enough.

BENEDICK Not I, believe me.   120

BEATRICE Did he never make you laugh?

BENEDICK I pray you, what is he?

BEATRICE Why, he is the Prince's jester, a very dull fool;
only his gift is in devising impossible slanders. None but
libertines delight in him, and the commendation is not
in his wit, but in his villainy; for he both pleases men
and angers them, and then they laugh at him and beat
him. I am sure he is in the fleet; I would he had boarded
me.

BENEDICK When I know the gentleman, I'll tell him what   130
you say.

BEATRICE Do, do; he'll but break a comparison or two
on me, which, peradventure not marked or not laughed
at, strikes him into melancholy; and then there's a
partridge wing saved, for the fool will eat no supper
that night.

Music for the dance
We must follow the leaders.

BENEDICK In every good thing.

53

BEATRICE Nay, if they lead to any ill, I will leave them at
140 the next turning.

Exeunt all dancing, except Don John,
Borachio, and Claudio

DON JOHN Sure my brother is amorous on Hero and hath
withdrawn her father to break with him about it. The
ladies follow her and but one visor remains.

BORACHIO And that is Claudio; I know him by his
bearing.

DON JOHN Are not you Signor Benedick?

CLAUDIO You know me well; I am he.

DON JOHN Signor, you are very near my brother in his
love. He is enamoured on Hero; I pray you dissuade
150 him from her; she is no equal for his birth. You may
do the part of an honest man in it.

CLAUDIO How know you he loves her?

DON JOHN I heard him swear his affection.

BORACHIO So did I too, and he swore he would marry her
tonight.

DON JOHN Come, let us to the banquet.

Exeunt Don John and Borachio

CLAUDIO
Thus answer I in name of Benedick,
But hear these ill news with the ears of Claudio.
'Tis certain so; the Prince woos for himself.
160 Friendship is constant in all other things
Save in the office and affairs of love;
Therefore all hearts in love use their own tongues.
Let every eye negotiate for itself,
And trust no agent; for beauty is a witch
Against whose charms faith melteth into blood.
This is an accident of hourly proof,
Which I mistrusted not. Farewell therefore, Hero!

Enter Benedick

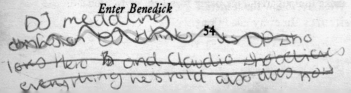

54

BENEDICK Count Claudio?

CLAUDIO Yea, the same.

BENEDICK Come, will you go with me? 170

CLAUDIO Whither?

BENEDICK Even to the next willow, about your own business, County. What fashion will you wear the garland
of? About your neck, like an usurer's chain? Or under
your arm, like a lieutenant's scarf? You must wear it
one way, for the Prince hath got your Hero.

CLAUDIO I wish him joy of her.

BENEDICK Why, that's spoken like an honest drovier; so
they sell bullocks. But did you think the Prince would
have served you thus? 180

CLAUDIO I pray you, leave me.

BENEDICK Ho! Now you strike like the blind man; 'twas
the boy that stole your meat, and you'll beat the post.

CLAUDIO If it will not be, I'll leave you. *Exit*

BENEDICK Alas, poor hurt fowl, now will he creep into
sedges! But that my Lady Beatrice should know me,
and not know me! The Prince's fool! Ha? It may be I
go under that title because I am merry. Yea, but so I am
apt to do myself wrong. I am not so reputed; it is the
base, though bitter, disposition of Beatrice that puts the 190
world into her person, and so gives me out. Well, I'll be
revenged as I may.

Enter Don Pedro, with Leonato and Hero

DON PEDRO Now, signor, where's the Count? Did you
see him?

BENEDICK Troth, my lord, I have played the part of Lady
Fame. I found him here as melancholy as a lodge in a
warren; I told him, and I think I told him true, that
your grace had got the good will of this young lady; and
I offered him my company to a willow-tree, either to
make him a garland, as being forsaken, or to bind him 200

up a rod, as being worthy to be whipped.

DON PEDRO To be whipped! What's his fault?

BENEDICK The flat transgression of a schoolboy, who, being overjoyed with finding a bird's nest, shows it his companion, and he steals it.

DON PEDRO Wilt thou make a trust a transgression? The transgression is in the stealer.

BENEDICK Yet it had not been amiss the rod had been made, and the garland too; for the garland he might
210   have worn himself, and the rod he might have bestowed on you, who, as I take it, have stolen his bird's nest.

DON PEDRO I will but teach them to sing, and restore them to the owner.

BENEDICK If their singing answer your saying, by my faith you say honestly.

DON PEDRO The Lady Beatrice hath a quarrel to you; the gentleman that danced with her told her she is much wronged by you.

BENEDICK O, she misused me past the endurance of a
220   block! An oak but with one green leaf on it would have answered her; my very visor began to assume life and scold with her. She told me, not thinking I had been myself, that I was the Prince's jester, that I was duller than a great thaw; huddling jest upon jest with such impossible conveyance upon me that I stood like a man at a mark, with a whole army shooting at me. She speaks poniards, and every word stabs. If her breath were as terrible as her terminations, there were no living near her; she would infect to the north star. I would not
230   marry her, though she were endowed with all that Adam had left him before he transgressed. She would have made Hercules have turned spit, yea, and have cleft his club to make the fire too. Come, talk not of her; you shall find her the infernal Ate in good apparel. I would to

God some scholar would conjure her; for certainly, while she is here, a man may live as quiet in hell as in a sanctuary, and people sin upon purpose, because they would go thither; so, indeed, all disquiet, horror, and perturbation follows her.

Enter Claudio and Beatrice

DON PEDRO Look, here she comes.   240

BENEDICK Will your grace command me any service to the world's end? I will go on the slightest errand now to the Antipodes that you can devise to send me on. I will fetch you a tooth-picker now from the furthest inch of Asia; bring you the length of Prester John's foot; fetch you a hair off the great Cham's beard; do you any embassage to the Pigmies, rather than hold three words' conference with this harpy. You have no employment for me?

DON PEDRO None, but to desire your good company.   250

BENEDICK O God, sir, here's a dish I love not; I cannot endure my Lady Tongue.   *Exit*

DON PEDRO Come, lady, come; you have lost the heart of Signor Benedick.

BEATRICE Indeed, my lord, he lent it me awhile, and I gave him use for it, a double heart for his single one. Marry, once before he won it of me with false dice, therefore your grace may well say I have lost it.

DON PEDRO You have put him down, lady, you have put him down.   260

BEATRICE So I would not he should do me, my lord, lest I should prove the mother of fools. I have brought Count Claudio, whom you sent me to seek.

DON PEDRO Why, how now, Count! Wherefore are you sad?

CLAUDIO Not sad, my lord.

DON PEDRO How then? Sick?

CLAUDIO Neither, my lord.

BEATRICE The Count is neither sad, nor sick, nor merry,
270 nor well; but civil count, civil as an orange, and something of that jealous complexion.

DON PEDRO I'faith, lady, I think your blazon to be true, though, I'll be sworn, if he be so, his conceit is false. Here, Claudio, I have wooed in thy name, and fair Hero is won. I have broke with her father, and his will obtained; name the day of marriage, and God give thee joy!

LEONATO Count, take of me my daughter, and with her my fortunes. His grace hath made the match, and all
280 Grace say Amen to it!

BEATRICE Speak, Count, 'tis your cue.

CLAUDIO Silence is the perfectest herald of joy; I were but little happy, if I could say how much. Lady, as you are mine, I am yours; I give away myself for you and dote upon the exchange.

BEATRICE Speak, cousin; or, if you cannot, stop his mouth with a kiss, and let not him speak neither.

DON PEDRO In faith, lady, you have a merry heart.

BEATRICE Yea, my lord; I thank it, poor fool, it keeps on
290 the windy side of care. My cousin tells him in his ear that he is in her heart.

CLAUDIO And so she doth, cousin.

BEATRICE Good Lord, for alliance! Thus goes every one to the world but I, and I am sunburnt; I may sit in a corner and cry 'Heigh-ho for a husband'!

DON PEDRO Lady Beatrice, I will get you one.

BEATRICE I would rather have one of your father's getting. Hath your grace ne'er a brother like you? Your father got excellent husbands, if a maid could come by
300 them.

DON PEDRO Will you have me, lady?

BEATRICE No, my lord, unless I might have another for working-days: your grace is too costly to wear every day. But, I beseech your grace, pardon me; I was born to speak all mirth and no matter.

DON PEDRO Your silence most offends me, and to be merry best becomes you; for, out o'question, you were born in a merry hour.

BEATRICE No, sure, my lord, my mother cried; but then there was a star danced, and under that was I born. 310 Cousins, God give you joy!

LEONATO Niece, will you look to those things I told you of?

BEATRICE I cry you mercy, uncle. *(To Don Pedro)* By your grace's pardon. *Exit*

DON PEDRO By my troth, a pleasant-spirited lady.

LEONATO There's little of the melancholy element in her, my lord; she is never sad but when she sleeps, and not ever sad then; for I have heard my daughter say, she hath often dreamt of unhappiness and waked herself with 320 laughing.

DON PEDRO She cannot endure to hear tell of a husband.

LEONATO O, by no means; she mocks all her wooers out of suit.

DON PEDRO She were an excellent wife for Benedick.

LEONATO O Lord, my lord, if they were but a week married, they would talk themselves mad.

DON PEDRO County Claudio, when mean you to go to church?

CLAUDIO Tomorrow, my lord. Time goes on crutches 330 till love have all his rites.

LEONATO Not till Monday, my dear son, which is hence a just seven-night; and a time too brief, too, to have all things answer my mind.

DON PEDRO Come, you shake the head at so long a

breathing; but, I warrant thee, Claudio, the time shall
not go dully by us. I will in the interim undertake one
of Hercules' labours; which is, to bring Signor Benedick
and the Lady Beatrice into a mountain of affection,
th'one with th'other. I would fain have it a match, and
I doubt not but to fashion it, if you three will but
minister such assistance as I shall give you direction.

LEONATO My lord, I am for you, though it cost me ten
nights' watchings.

CLAUDIO And I, my lord.

DON PEDRO And you too, gentle Hero?

HERO I will do any modest office, my lord, to help my
cousin to a good husband.

DON PEDRO And Benedick is not the unhopefullest husband that I know. Thus far can I praise him: he is of a
noble strain, of approved valour and confirmed honesty.
I will teach you how to humour your cousin, that she
shall fall in love with Benedick; and I, with your two
helps, will so practise on Benedick that, in despite of
his quick wit and his queasy stomach, he shall fall in
love with Beatrice. If we can do this, Cupid is no
longer an archer; his glory shall be ours, for we are the
only love-gods. Go in with me, and I will tell you my
drift.   *Exeunt*

II.2   *Enter Don John and Borachio*

DON JOHN It is so; the Count Claudio shall marry the
daughter of Leonato.

BORACHIO Yea, my lord, but I can cross it.

DON JOHN Any bar, any cross, any impediment will be
medicinable to me: I am sick in displeasure to him,
and whatsoever comes athwart his affection ranges
evenly with mine. How canst thou cross this marriage?

BORACHIO Not honestly, my lord; but so covertly that no dishonesty shall appear in me.

DON JOHN Show me briefly how.　　　　　　　　　　　　10

BORACHIO I think I told your lordship a year since, how much I am in the favour of Margaret, the waiting-gentlewoman to Hero.

DON JOHN I remember.

BORACHIO I can, at any unseasonable instant of the night, appoint her to look out at her lady's chamber-window.

DON JOHN What life is in that, to be the death of this marriage?

BORACHIO The poison of that lies in you to temper. Go you to the Prince your brother; spare not to tell him　20 that he hath wronged his honour in marrying the renowned Claudio – whose estimation do you mightily hold up – to a contaminated stale, such a one as Hero.

DON JOHN What proof shall I make of that?

BORACHIO Proof enough to misuse the Prince, to vex Claudio, to undo Hero and kill Leonato. Look you for any other issue?

DON JOHN Only to despite them I will endeavour anything.

BORACHIO Go, then; find me a meet hour to draw Don　30 Pedro and the Count Claudio alone. Tell them that you know that Hero loves me; intend a kind of zeal both to the Prince and Claudio – as in love of your brother's honour, who hath made this match, and his friend's reputation, who is thus like to be cozened with the semblance of a maid – that you have discovered thus. They will scarcely believe this without trial; offer them instances, which shall bear no less likelihood than to see me at her chamber window, hear me call Margaret Hero, hear Margaret term me Claudio; and bring them　40 to see this the very night before the intended wedding –

61

for in the meantime I will so fashion the matter that
Hero shall be absent – and there shall appear such seeming truth of Hero's disloyalty that jealousy shall be called
assurance, and all the preparation overthrown.

DON JOHN Grow this to what adverse issue it can, I will
put it in practice. Be cunning in the working this, and
thy fee is a thousand ducats.

BORACHIO Be you constant in the accusation, and my
50   cunning shall not shame me.

DON JOHN I will presently go learn their day of marriage.

Exeunt

II.3   *Enter Benedick alone*

BENEDICK Boy!

        Enter Boy

BOY Signor?

BENEDICK In my chamber-window lies a book; bring it
hither to me in the orchard.

BOY I am here already, sir.

BENEDICK I know that; but I would have thee hence, and
here again.   *Exit Boy*

I do much wonder that one man, seeing how much
another man is a fool when he dedicates his behaviours
10 to love, will, after he hath laughed at such shallow
follies in others, become the argument of his own
scorn by falling in love; and such a man is Claudio. I
have known when there was no music with him but the
drum and the fife, and now had he rather hear the tabor
and the pipe. I have known when he would have walked
ten mile afoot to see a good armour, and now will he lie
ten nights awake carving the fashion of a new doublet.
He was wont to speak plain and to the purpose, like an
honest man and a soldier, and now is he turned ortho-
20 graphy; his words are a very fantastical banquet, just so

62

many strange dishes. May I be so converted and see with
these eyes? I cannot tell; I think not. I will not be
sworn but love may transform me to an oyster; but I'll
take my oath on it, till he have made an oyster of me, he
shall never make me such a fool. One woman is fair, yet
I am well; another is wise, yet I am well; another virtuous, yet I am well; but till all graces be in one woman,
one woman shall not come in my grace. Rich she shall
be, that's certain; wise, or I'll none; virtuous, or I'll
never cheapen her; fair, or I'll never look on her; mild, 30
or come not near me; noble, or not I for an angel; of
good discourse, an excellent musician, and her hair shall
be of what colour it please God. Ha! The Prince and
Monsieur Love! I will hide me in the arbour.

He withdraws
Enter Don Pedro, Leonato, and Claudio

DON PEDRO
Come, shall we hear this music?

CLAUDIO
Yea, my good lord. How still the evening is,
As hushed on purpose to grace harmony!

DON PEDRO
See you where Benedick hath hid himself?

CLAUDIO
O, very well, my lord; the music ended,
We'll fit the hid-fox with a pennyworth. 40

Enter Balthasar with music

DON PEDRO
Come, Balthasar, we'll hear that song again.

BALTHASAR
O, good my lord, tax not so bad a voice
To slander music any more than once.

DON PEDRO
It is the witness still of excellency

63

To put a strange face on his own perfection.
I pray thee sing, and let me woo no more.

BALTHASAR
Because you talk of wooing, I will sing,
Since many a wooer doth commence his suit
To her he thinks not worthy; yet he woos,
50 Yet will he swear he loves.

DON PEDRO   Nay, pray thee, come;
Or, if thou wilt hold longer argument,
Do it in notes.

BALTHASAR   Note this before my notes;
There's not a note of mine that's worth the noting.

DON PEDRO
Why, these are very crotchets that he speaks;
Note notes, forsooth, and nothing.
              Music

BENEDICK Now, divine air! Now is his soul ravished! Is
it not strange that sheep's guts should hale souls out of
men's bodies? Well, a horn for my money, when all's
done.   *The Song*

BALTHASAR
60   Sigh no more, ladies, sigh no more,
                 Men were deceivers ever,
           One foot in sea and one on shore,
                 To one thing constant never:
           Then sigh not so, but let them go,
                 And be you blithe and bonny,
           Converting all your sounds of woe
                 Into Hey nonny, nonny.

           Sing no more ditties, sing no moe,
                 Of dumps so dull and heavy;
70   The fraud of men was ever so,
                 Since summer first was leavy:
           Then sigh not so, but let them go,

> And be you blithe and bonny,
> Converting all your sounds of woe
> Into Hey nonny, nonny.

DON PEDRO By my troth, a good song.

BALTHASAR And an ill singer, my lord.

DON PEDRO Ha, no, no, faith; thou singest well enough
for a shift.

BENEDICK An he had been a dog that should have 80
howled thus, they would have hanged him; and I pray
God his bad voice bode no mischief. I had as lief have
heard the night-raven, come what plague could have
come after it.

DON PEDRO Yea, marry, dost thou hear, Balthasar? I
pray thee, get us some excellent music; for tomorrow
night we would have it at the Lady Hero's chamber-
window.

BALTHASAR The best I can, my lord.

DON PEDRO Do so; farewell. *Exit Balthasar* 90
Come hither, Leonato. What was it you told me of to-
day, that your niece Beatrice was in love with Signor
Benedick?

CLAUDIO (*aside*) O, ay; stalk on, stalk on, the fowl sits. – I
did never think that lady would have loved any man.

LEONATO No, nor I neither; but most wonderful that
she should dote so on Signor Benedick, whom she hath
in all outward behaviours seemed ever to abhor.

BENEDICK (*aside*) Is't possible? Sits the wind in that
corner? 100

LEONATO By my troth, my lord, I cannot tell what to
think of it; but that she loves him with an enraged affection, it is past the infinite of thought.

DON PEDRO May be she doth but counterfeit.

CLAUDIO Faith, like enough.

LEONATO O God! Counterfeit? There was never counterfeit of passion came so near the life of passion as she discovers it.

DON PEDRO Why, what effects of passion shows she?

110 CLAUDIO (*to Don Pedro and Leonato*) Bait the hook well; this fish will bite.

LEONATO What effects, my lord? She will sit you – you heard my daughter tell you how.

CLAUDIO She did, indeed.

DON PEDRO How, how, I pray you? You amaze me; I would have thought her spirit had been invincible against all assaults of affection.

LEONATO I would have sworn it had, my lord, especially against Benedick.

120 BENEDICK (*aside*) I should think this a gull, but that the white-bearded fellow speaks it; knavery cannot, sure, hide himself in such reverence.

CLAUDIO (*to Don Pedro and Leonato*) He hath ta'en the infection; hold it up.

DON PEDRO Hath she made her affection known to Benedick?

LEONATO No, and swears she never will; that's her torment.

CLAUDIO 'Tis true, indeed, so your daughter says. 'Shall 130 I,' says she, 'that have so oft encountered him with scorn, write to him that I love him?'

LEONATO This says she now when she is beginning to write to him; for she'll be up twenty times a night, and there will she sit in her smock till she have writ a sheet of paper. My daughter tells us all.

CLAUDIO Now you talk of a sheet of paper, I remember a pretty jest your daughter told us of.

LEONATO O, when she had writ it and was reading it over, she found Benedick and Beatrice between the 140 sheet?

CLAUDIO That.

LEONATO O, she tore the letter into a thousand halfpence; railed at herself, that she should be so immodest to write to one that she knew would flout her.
'I measure him,' says she, 'by my own spirit; for I
should flout him, if he writ to me; yea, though I love
him, I should.'

CLAUDIO Then down upon her knees she falls, weeps,
sobs, beats her heart, tears her hair, prays, curses – 'O
sweet Benedick! God give me patience!'   150

LEONATO She doth indeed, my daughter says so; and the
ecstasy hath so much overborne her that my daughter
is sometime afeard she will do a desperate outrage to
herself. It is very true.

DON PEDRO It were good that Benedick knew of it by
some other, if she will not discover it.

CLAUDIO To what end? He would make but a sport of it
and torment the poor lady worse.

DON PEDRO An he should, it were an alms to hang him.
She's an excellent sweet lady, and, out of all suspicion, 160
she is virtuous.

CLAUDIO And she is exceeding wise.

DON PEDRO In every thing but in loving Benedick.

LEONATO O, my lord, wisdom and blood combating in so
tender a body, we have ten proofs to one that blood
hath the victory. I am sorry for her, as I have just cause,
being her uncle and her guardian.

DON PEDRO I would she had bestowed this dotage on me;
I would have daffed all other respects and made her half
myself. I pray you, tell Benedick of it, and hear what 170
'a will say.

LEONATO Were it good, think you?

CLAUDIO Hero thinks surely she will die; for she says she
will die, if he love her not; and she will die, ere she make

her love known; and she will die if he woo her, rather than she will bate one breath of her accustomed crossness.

DON PEDRO She doth well. If she should make tender of her love, 'tis very possible he'll scorn it; for the man,
180 as you know all, hath a contemptible spirit.

CLAUDIO He is a very proper man.

DON PEDRO He hath, indeed, a good outward happiness.

CLAUDIO Before God, and in my mind, very wise.

DON PEDRO He doth, indeed, show some sparks that are like wit.

CLAUDIO And I take him to be valiant.

DON PEDRO As Hector, I assure you; and in the managing of quarrels you may say he is wise, for either he avoids them with great discretion, or undertakes them
190 with a most Christian-like fear.

LEONATO If he do fear God, 'a must necessarily keep peace; if he break the peace, he ought to enter into a quarrel with fear and trembling.

DON PEDRO And so will he do, for the man doth fear God, howsoever it seems not in him by some large jests he will make. Well, I am sorry for your niece. Shall we go seek Benedick, and tell him of her love?

CLAUDIO Never tell him, my lord; let her wear it out with good counsel.

200 LEONATO Nay, that's impossible; she may wear her heart out first.

DON PEDRO Well, we will hear further of it by your daughter; let it cool the while. I love Benedick well; and I could wish he would modestly examine himself, to see how much he is unworthy so good a lady.

LEONATO My lord, will you walk? Dinner is ready.

CLAUDIO (aside) If he do not dote on her upon this, I will never trust my expectation.

DON PEDRO (*to Leonato*) Let there be the same net spread
for her, and that must your daughter and her gentle- 210
women carry. The sport will be, when they hold one
an opinion of another's dotage, and no such matter;
that's the scene that I would see, which will be merely a
dumb-show. Let us send her to call him in to dinner.
     Exeunt Don Pedro, Claudio, and Leonato
BENEDICK (*coming forward*) This can be no trick. The
conference was sadly borne. They have the truth of this
from Hero. They seem to pity the lady; it seems her
affections have their full bent. Love me? Why, it must
be requited. I heard how I am censured: they say I will
bear myself proudly, if I perceive the love come from 220
her; they say, too, that she will rather die than give any
sign of affection. I did never think to marry. I must not
seem proud; happy are they that hear their detractions
and can put them to mending. They say the lady is fair;
'tis a truth, I can bear them witness; and virtuous; so,
I cannot reprove it; and wise, but for loving me. By my
troth, it is no addition to her wit, nor no great argument
of her folly, for I will be horribly in love with her. I may
chance have some odd quirks and remnants of wit broken
on me, because I have railed so long against marriage; 230
but doth not the appetite alter? A man loves the meat in
his youth that he cannot endure in his age. Shall quips
and sentences and these paper bullets of the brain awe a
man from the career of his humour? No, the world must
be peopled. When I said I would die a bachelor, I did
not think I should live till I were married. Here comes
Beatrice. By this day, she's a fair lady! I do spy some
marks of love in her.
  Enter Beatrice
BEATRICE Against my will I am sent to bid you come in to
dinner. 240

BENEDICK

Fair Beatrice, I thank you for your pains.

BEATRICE I took no more pains for those thanks than
you take pains to thank me; if it had been painful, I
would not have come.

BENEDICK You take pleasure then in the message?

BEATRICE Yea, just so much as you may take upon a
knife's point, and choke a daw withal. You have no
stomach, signor; fare you well.   *Exit*

BENEDICK Ha! 'Against my will I am sent to bid you
250   come in to dinner' – there's a double meaning in that. 'I
took no more pains for those thanks than you took pains
to thank me' – that's as much as to say, 'Any pains that
I take for you is as easy as thanks.' If I do not take pity of
her, I am a villain; if I do not love her, I am a Jew. I will
go get her picture.   *Exit*

*

III.1   *Enter Hero and two gentlewomen (Margaret and Ursula)*

HERO

Good Margaret, run thee to the parlour;
There shalt thou find my cousin Beatrice
Proposing with the Prince and Claudio.
Whisper her ear, and tell her I and Ursula
Walk in the orchard, and our whole discourse
Is all of her; say that thou overheardst us,
And bid her steal into the pleachèd bower,
Where honeysuckles, ripened by the sun,
Forbid the sun to enter – like favourites,
10   Made proud by princes, that advance their pride
Against that power that bred it. There will she hide her,
To listen our propose. This is thy office;

Bear thee well in it, and leave us alone.

MARGARET

I'll make her come, I warrant you, presently.   *Exit*

HERO

Now, Ursula, when Beatrice doth come,
As we do trace this alley up and down,
Our talk must only be of Benedick;
When I do name him, let it be thy part
To praise him more than ever man did merit.
My talk to thee must be how Benedick   20
Is sick in love with Beatrice. Of this matter
Is little Cupid's crafty arrow made,
That only wounds by hearsay. Now begin;

Enter Beatrice secretively. She slips into the bower

For look where Beatrice, like a lapwing, runs
Close by the ground, to hear our conference.

URSULA (*to Hero*)

The pleasant'st angling is to see the fish
Cut with her golden oars the silver stream,
And greedily devour the treacherous bait;
So angle we for Beatrice, who even now
Is couchèd in the woodbine coverture.   30
Fear you not my part of the dialogue.

HERO (*to Ursula*)

Then go we near her, that her ear lose nothing
Of the false sweet bait that we lay for it.

They approach the bower

No, truly, Ursula, she is too disdainful;
I know her spirits are as coy and wild
As haggards of the rock.

URSULA   But are you sure
That Benedick loves Beatrice so entirely?

HERO

So says the Prince and my new-trothèd lord.

71

III.1

URSULA

And did they bid you tell her of it, madam?

HERO

40 They did entreat me to acquaint her of it;
But I persuaded them, if they loved Benedick,
To wish him wrestle with affection,
And never to let Beatrice know of it.

URSULA

Why did you so? Doth not the gentleman
Deserve as full as fortunate a bed
As ever Beatrice shall couch upon?

HERO

O god of love! I know he doth deserve
As much as may be yielded to a man;
But Nature never framed a woman's heart
50 Of prouder stuff than that of Beatrice.
Disdain and scorn ride sparkling in her eyes,
Misprizing what they look on, and her wit
Values itself so highly that to her
All matter else seems weak. She cannot love,
Nor take no shape nor project of affection,
She is so self-endeared.

URSULA   Sure, I think so;
And therefore, certainly, it were not good
She knew his love, lest she'll make sport at it.

HERO

Why, you speak truth. I never yet saw man,
60 How wise, how noble, young, how rarely featured,
But she would spell him backward. If fair-faced,
She would swear the gentleman should be her sister;
If black, why, Nature, drawing of an antic,
Made a foul blot; if tall, a lance ill-headed;
If low, an agate very vilely cut;
If speaking, why, a vane blown with all winds;
If silent, why, a block movèd with none.

So turns she every man the wrong side out,
And never gives to truth and virtue that
Which simpleness and merit purchaseth.   70

URSULA
Sure, sure, such carping is not commendable.

HERO
No, not to be so odd and from all fashions
As Beatrice is, cannot be commendable;
But who dare tell her so? If I should speak,
She would mock me into air; O, she would laugh me
Out of myself, press me to death with wit!
Therefore let Benedick, like covered fire,
Consume away in sighs, waste inwardly.
It were a better death than die with mocks,
Which is as bad as die with tickling.   80

URSULA
Yet tell her of it; hear what she will say.

HERO
No; rather I will go to Benedick
And counsel him to fight against his passion.
And, truly, I'll devise some honest slanders
To stain my cousin with. One doth not know
How much an ill word may empoison liking.

URSULA
O, do not do your cousin such a wrong!
She cannot be so much without true judgement –
Having so swift and excellent a wit
As she is prized to have – as to refuse   90
So rare a gentleman as Signor Benedick.

HERO
He is the only man of Italy,
Always excepted my dear Claudio.

URSULA
I pray you be not angry with me, madam,
Speaking my fancy; Signor Benedick,

For shape, for bearing, argument and valour,
Goes foremost in report through Italy.

HERO

Indeed, he hath an excellent good name.

URSULA

His excellence did earn it ere he had it.
100 When are you married, madam?

HERO

Why, every day, tomorrow. Come, go in;
I'll show thee some attires, and have thy counsel
Which is the best to furnish me tomorrow.

URSULA (to Hero)

She's limed, I warrant you; we have caught her, madam.

HERO (to Ursula)

If it prove so, then loving goes by haps;
Some Cupid kills with arrows, some with traps.

Exeunt Hero and Ursula

BEATRICE (coming forward)

What fire is in mine ears? Can this be true?
Stand I condemned for pride and scorn so much?
Contempt, farewell! and maiden pride, adieu!
110 No glory lives behind the back of such.
And, Benedick, love on; I will requite thee,
Taming my wild heart to thy loving hand.
If thou dost love, my kindness shall incite thee
To bind our loves up in a holy band.
For others say thou dost deserve, and I
Believe it better than reportingly.

Exit

III.2   *Enter Don Pedro, Claudio, Benedick, and Leonato*

DON PEDRO I do but stay till your marriage be consum-
mate, and then go I toward Arragon.

CLAUDIO I'll bring you thither, my lord, if you'll vouchsafe me.

DON PEDRO Nay, that would be as great a soil in the new gloss of your marriage as to show a child his new coat and forbid him to wear it. I will only be bold with Benedick for his company; for, from the crown of his head to the sole of his foot, he is all mirth; he hath twice or thrice cut Cupid's bow-string and the little hangman 10 dare not shoot at him. He hath a heart as sound as a bell and his tongue is the clapper, for what his heart thinks, his tongue speaks.

BENEDICK Gallants, I am not as I have been.

LEONATO So say I; methinks you are sadder.

CLAUDIO I hope he be in love.

DON PEDRO Hang him, truant! There's no true drop of blood in him to be truly touched with love; if he be sad, he wants money.

BENEDICK I have the toothache. 20

DON PEDRO Draw it.

BENEDICK Hang it!

CLAUDIO You must hang it first, and draw it afterwards.

DON PEDRO What! Sigh for the toothache?

LEONATO Where is but a humour or a worm.

BENEDICK Well, everyone can master a grief but he that has it.

CLAUDIO Yet say I, he is in love.

DON PEDRO There is no appearance of fancy in him, unless it be a fancy that he hath to strange disguises; as to 30 be a Dutchman today, a Frenchman tomorrow, or in the shape of two countries at once, as, a German from the waist downward, all slops, and a Spaniard from the hip upward, no doublet. Unless he have a fancy to this foolery, as it appears he hath, he is no fool for fancy, as you would have it appear he is.

CLAUDIO If he be not in love with some woman, there is
no believing old signs. 'A brushes his hat o'mornings;
what should that bode?

40 DON PEDRO Hath any man seen him at the barber's?

CLAUDIO No, but the barber's man hath been seen with
him and the old ornament of his cheek hath already
stuffed tennis-balls.

LEONATO Indeed, he looks younger than he did, by the
loss of a beard.

DON PEDRO Nay, 'a rubs himself with civet; can you smell
him out by that?

CLAUDIO That's as much as to say, the sweet youth's in
love.

50 DON PEDRO The greatest note of it is his melancholy.

CLAUDIO And when was he wont to wash his face?

DON PEDRO Yea, or to paint himself? For the which, I hear
what they say of him.

CLAUDIO Nay, but his jesting spirit, which is now crept
into a lute-string and now governed by stops.

DON PEDRO Indeed, that tells a heavy tale for him; conclude, conclude he is in love.

CLAUDIO Nay, but I know who loves him.

DON PEDRO That would I know too; I warrant, one that
60 knows him not.

CLAUDIO Yes, and his ill conditions; and, in despite of all,
dies for him.

DON PEDRO She shall be buried with her face upwards.

BENEDICK Yet is this no charm for the toothache. Old
signor, walk aside with me; I have studied eight or nine
wise words to speak to you, which these hobby-horses
must not hear.   *Exeunt Benedick and Leonato*

DON PEDRO For my life, to break with him about Beatrice.

CLAUDIO 'Tis even so. Hero and Margaret have by this
70 played their parts with Beatrice, and then the two bears

will not bite one another when they meet.

Enter Don John

DON JOHN My lord and brother, God save you!

DON PEDRO Good-e'en, brother.

DON JOHN If your leisure served, I would speak with you.

DON PEDRO In private?

DON JOHN If it please you; yet Count Claudio may hear,
for what I would speak of concerns him.

DON PEDRO What's the matter?

DON JOHN (*to Claudio*) Means your lordship to be
married tomorrow?   80

DON PEDRO You know he does.

DON JOHN I know not that, when he knows what I know.

CLAUDIO If there be any impediment, I pray you discover
it.

DON JOHN You may think I love you not; let that appear
hereafter, and aim better at me by that I now will
manifest. For my brother, I think he holds you well,
and in dearness of heart hath holp to effect your ensuing
marriage – surely suit ill spent, and labour ill bestowed!

DON PEDRO Why, what's the matter?   90

DON JOHN I came hither to tell you; and, circumstances
shortened, for she has been too long a talking of, the
lady is disloyal.

CLAUDIO Who, Hero?

DON JOHN Even she – Leonato's Hero, your Hero, every
man's Hero.

CLAUDIO Disloyal?

DON JOHN The word is too good to paint out her wicked-
ness. I could say she were worse; think you of a worse
title, and I will fit her to it. Wonder not till further   100
warrant. Go but with me tonight, you shall see her
chamber-window entered, even the night before her
wedding-day. If you love her then, tomorrow wed her;

77

but it would better fit your honour to change your mind.

CLAUDIO May this be so?

DON PEDRO I will not think it.

DON JOHN If you dare not trust that you see, confess not that you know. If you will follow me, I will show you enough; and when you have seen more and heard more, proceed accordingly.

CLAUDIO If I see any thing tonight why I should not marry her, tomorrow in the congregation, where I should wed, there will I shame her.

DON PEDRO And, as I wooed for thee to obtain her, I will join with thee to disgrace her.

DON JOHN I will disparage her no farther till you are my witness; bear it coldly but till midnight, and let the issue show itself.

DON PEDRO O day untowardly turned!

CLAUDIO O mischief strangely thwarting!

DON JOHN O plague right well prevented! So will you say when you have seen the sequel.

Exeunt

III.3   *Enter Dogberry and his compartner Verges with the Watch*

DOGBERRY Are you good men and true?

VERGES Yea, or else it were pity but they should suffer salvation, body and soul.

DOGBERRY Nay, that were a punishment too good for them, if they should have any allegiance in them, being chosen for the Prince's watch.

VERGES Well, give them their charge, neighbour Dogberry.

DOGBERRY First, who think you the most desartless man to be constable?

78

FIRST WATCHMAN Hugh Oatcake, sir, or George Seacoal, for they can write and read.

DOGBERRY Come hither, neighbour Seacoal. God hath blessed you with a good name. To be a well-favoured man is the gift of fortune; but to write and read comes by nature.

SECOND WATCHMAN Both which, Master Constable—

DOGBERRY You have; I knew it would be your answer. Well, for your favour, sir, why, give God thanks, and make no boast of it; and for your writing and reading, 20 let that appear when there is no need of such vanity. You are thought here to be the most senseless and fit man for the constable of the watch; therefore bear you the lantern. This is your charge: you shall comprehend all vagrom men; you are to bid any man stand, in the Prince's name.

SECOND WATCHMAN How if 'a will not stand?

DOGBERRY Why, then, take no note of him, but let him go; and presently call the rest of the watch together and thank God you are rid of a knave. 30

VERGES If he will not stand when he is bidden, he is none of the Prince's subjects.

DOGBERRY True, and they are to meddle with none but the Prince's subjects. You shall also make no noise in the streets; for for the watch to babble and to talk is most tolerable and not to be endured.

FIRST WATCHMAN We will rather sleep than talk; we know what belongs to a watch.

DOGBERRY Why, you speak like an ancient and most quiet watchman, for I cannot see how sleeping should offend; 40 only, have a care that your bills be not stolen. Well, you are to call at all the ale-houses, and bid those that are drunk get them to bed.

SECOND WATCHMAN How if they will not?

DOGBERRY Why, then, let them alone till they are sober;
if they make you not then the better answer, you may
say they are not the men you took them for.

SECOND WATCHMAN Well, sir.

DOGBERRY If you meet a thief, you may suspect him, by
50 virtue of your office, to be no true man; and, for such
kind of men, the less you meddle or make with them,
why, the more is for your honesty.

SECOND WATCHMAN If we know him to be a thief, shall
we not lay hands on him?

DOGBERRY Truly, by your office, you may, but I think
they that touch pitch will be defiled. The most peaceable way for you, if you do take a thief, is to let him
show himself what he is and steal out of your company.

VERGES You have been always called a merciful man,
60 partner.

DOGBERRY Truly, I would not hang a dog by my will,
much more a man who hath any honesty in him.

VERGES If you hear a child cry in the night, you must call
to the nurse and bid her still it.

SECOND WATCHMAN How if the nurse be asleep and will
not hear us?

DOGBERRY Why, then, depart in peace, and let the child
wake her with crying; for the ewe that will not hear her
lamb when it baes will never answer a calf when he
70 bleats.

VERGES 'Tis very true.

DOGBERRY This is the end of the charge: you, constable,
are to present the Prince's own person; if you meet the
Prince in the night, you may stay him.

VERGES Nay, by'r Lady, that I think 'a cannot.

DOGBERRY Five shillings to one on't, with any man that
knows the statutes, he may stay him; marry, not without
the Prince be willing; for, indeed, the watch ought to

offend no man, and it is an offence to stay a man against
his will.   80

VERGES By'r Lady, I think it be so.

DOGBERRY Ha, ah ha! Well, masters, good night; an
there be any matter of weight chances, call up me. Keep
your fellows' counsels and your own, and good night.
Come, neighbour.

FIRST WATCHMAN Well, masters, we hear our charge.
Let us go sit here upon the church-bench till two, and
then all to bed.

DOGBERRY One word more, honest neighbours. I pray
you, watch about Signor Leonato's door, for the wed-   90
ding being there tomorrow, there is a great coil to-night.
Adieu; be vigitant, I beseech you.

Exeunt Dogberry and Verges

Enter Borachio and Conrade

BORACHIO What, Conrade!

SECOND WATCHMAN (*aside*) Peace! stir not.

BORACHIO Conrade, I say!

CONRADE Here, man, I am at thy elbow.

BORACHIO Mass, and my elbow itched; I thought there
would a scab follow.

CONRADE I will owe thee an answer for that; and now
forward with thy tale.   100

BORACHIO Stand thee close then under this pent-house,
for it drizzles rain; and I will, like a true drunkard,
utter all to thee.

SECOND WATCHMAN (*aside*) Some treason, masters; yet
stand close.

BORACHIO Therefore know I have earned of Don John a
thousand ducats.

CONRADE Is it possible that any villainy should be so dear?

BORACHIO Thou shouldst rather ask if it were possible
any villainy should be so rich; for when rich villains   110

81

have need of poor ones, poor ones may make what price they will.

CONRADE I wonder at it.

BORACHIO That shows thou art unconfirmed. Thou knowest that the fashion of a doublet, or a hat, or a cloak, is nothing to a man.

CONRADE Yes, it is apparel.

BORACHIO I mean, the fashion.

CONRADE Yes, the fashion is the fashion.

120 BORACHIO Tush! I may as well say the fool's the fool. But seest thou not what a deformed thief this fashion is?

FIRST WATCHMAN (*aside*) I know that Deformed; 'a has been a vile thief this seven year; 'a goes up and down like a gentleman. I remember his name.

BORACHIO Didst thou not hear somebody?

CONRADE No; 'twas the vane on the house.

BORACHIO Seest thou not, I say, what a deformed thief this fashion is, how giddily 'a turns about all the hot bloods between fourteen and five-and-thirty, some-
130 times fashioning them like Pharaoh's soldiers in the reechy painting, sometime like god Bel's priests in the old church-window, sometime like the shaven Hercules in the smirched worm-eaten tapestry, where his cod-piece seems as massy as his club?

CONRADE All this I see; and I see that the fashion wears out more apparel than the man. But art not thou thyself giddy with the fashion too, that thou hast shifted out of thy tale into telling me of the fashion?

BORACHIO Not so, neither: but know that I have tonight
140 wooed Margaret, the Lady Hero's gentlewoman, by the name of Hero; she leans me out at her mistress' chamber-window, bids me a thousand times good-night – I tell this tale vilely – I should first tell thee how the Prince, Claudio, and my master, planted, and

placed, and possessed, by my master Don John, saw afar
off in the orchard this amiable encounter.

CONRADE And thought they Margaret was Hero?

BORACHIO Two of them did, the Prince and Claudio; but
the devil my master knew she was Margaret; and partly
by his oaths, which first possessed them, partly by the 150
dark night, which did deceive them, but chiefly by my
villainy, which did confirm any slander that Don John
had made, away went Claudio enraged; swore he would
meet her, as he was appointed, next morning at the
temple, and there, before the whole congregation, shame
her with what he saw o'er night, and send her home
again without a husband.

FIRST WATCHMAN We charge you, in the Prince's name,
stand!

SECOND WATCHMAN Call up the right Master Constable. 160
We have here recovered the most dangerous piece of
lechery that ever was known in the commonwealth.

FIRST WATCHMAN And one Deformed is one of them; I
know him, 'a wears a lock.

CONRADE Masters, masters –

SECOND WATCHMAN You'll be made bring Deformed
forth, I warrant you.

CONRADE Masters –

FIRST WATCHMAN Never speak, we charge you; let us
obey you to go with us. 170

BORACHIO We are like to prove a goodly commodity,
being taken up of these men's bills.

CONRADE A commodity in question, I warrant you. Come,
we'll obey you.   *Exeunt*

83

Enter Hero, and Margaret, and Ursula

HERO Good Ursula, wake my cousin Beatrice, and desire
her to rise.

URSULA I will, lady.

HERO And bid her come hither.

URSULA Well.   *Exit*

MARGARET Troth, I think your other rebato were better.

HERO No, pray thee, good Meg, I'll wear this.

MARGARET By my troth, 's not so good, and I warrant
your cousin will say so.

10 HERO My cousin's a fool, and thou art another. I'll wear
none but this.

MARGARET I like the new tire within excellently, if the
hair were a thought browner; and your gown's a most
rare fashion, i'faith. I saw the Duchess of Milan's gown
that they praise so.

HERO O, that exceeds, they say.

MARGARET By my troth, 's but a nightgown in respect of
yours – cloth o'gold, and cuts, and laced with silver, set
with pearls, down-sleeves, side-sleeves, and skirts, round
20 underborne with a bluish tinsel; but for a fine, quaint,
graceful and excellent fashion, yours is worth ten on't.

HERO God give me joy to wear it, for my heart is exceed-
ingly heavy.

MARGARET 'Twill be heavier soon, by the weight of a man.

HERO Fie upon thee! Art not ashamed?

MARGARET Of what, lady? Of speaking honourably? Is
not marriage honourable in a beggar? Is not your lord
honourable without marriage? I think you would have
me say, 'saving your reverence, a husband'; an bad
30 thinking do not wrest true speaking, I'll offend nobody.
Is there any harm in 'the heavier for a husband'? None,
I think, an it be the right husband and the right wife;
otherwise 'tis light, and not heavy; ask my Lady

Beatrice else, here she comes.

Enter Beatrice

HERO Good morrow, coz.

BEATRICE Good morrow, sweet Hero.

HERO Why, how now? Do you speak in the sick tune?

BEATRICE I am out of all other tune, methinks.

MARGARET Clap's into 'Light o' love'; that goes without a
burden. Do you sing it, and I'll dance it.   40

BEATRICE Ye light o'love, with your heels! Then if your
husband have stables enough, you'll see he shall lack no
barnes.

MARGARET O illegitimate construction! I scorn that with
my heels.

BEATRICE 'Tis almost five o'clock, cousin; 'tis time you
were ready. By my troth, I am exceeding ill; heigh-ho!

MARGARET For a hawk, a horse, or a husband?

BEATRICE For the letter that begins them all, H.

MARGARET Well, an you be not turned Turk, there's no   50
more sailing by the star.

BEATRICE What means the fool, trow?

MARGARET Nothing I; but God send everyone their
heart's desire!

HERO These gloves the Count sent me; they are an excellent perfume.

BEATRICE I am stuffed, cousin, I cannot smell.

MARGARET A maid, and stuffed! There's goodly catching
of cold.

BEATRICE O, God help me! God help me! How long have   60
you professed apprehension?

MARGARET Ever since you left it. Doth not my wit
become me rarely?

BEATRICE It is not seen enough; you should wear it in
your cap. By my troth, I am sick.

MARGARET Get you some of this distilled Carduus Bene-

dictus, and lay it to your heart: it is the only thing for a
qualm.

HERO There thou prickest her with a thistle.

70 BEATRICE Benedictus! Why Benedictus? You have some
moral in this Benedictus.

MARGARET Moral? No, by my troth, I have no moral
meaning; I meant plain holy-thistle. You may think per-
chance that I think you are in love. Nay, by'r Lady, I
am not such a fool to think what I list, nor I list not to
think what I can, nor indeed I cannot think, if I would
think my heart out of thinking, that you are in love, or
that you will be in love, or that you can be in love. Yet
Benedick was such another, and now is he become a

80 man; he swore he would never marry, and yet now, in
despite of his heart, he eats his meat without grudging;
and how you may be converted I know not, but methinks you look with your eyes as other women do.

BEATRICE What pace is this that thy tongue keeps?

MARGARET Not a false gallop.

Enter Ursula

URSULA Madam, withdraw; the Prince, the Count, Signor
Benedick, Don John, and all the gallants of the town, are
come to fetch you to church.

HERO Help to dress me, good coz, good Meg, good
90 Ursula.   *Exeunt*

III.5   *Enter Leonato, with the Constable, Dogberry and the
            Headborough, Verges*

LEONATO What would you with me, honest neighbour?

DOGBERRY Marry, sir, I would have some confidence with
you that decerns you nearly.

LEONATO Brief, I pray you, for you see it is a busy time
with me.

DOGBERRY Marry, this it is, sir.

VERGES Yes, in truth it is, sir.

LEONATO What is it, my good friends?

DOGBERRY Goodman Verges, sir, speaks a little off the matter – an old man, sir, and his wits are not so blunt as, 10 God help, I would desire they were; but, in faith, honest as the skin between his brows.

VERGES Yes, I thank God I am as honest as any man living that is an old man and no honester than I.

DOGBERRY Comparisons are odorous; *palabras,* neighbour Verges.

LEONATO Neighbours, you are tedious.

DOGBERRY It pleases your worship to say so, but we are the poor Duke's officers; but truly, for mine own part, if I were as tedious as a king, I could find it in my heart to 20 bestow it all of your worship.

LEONATO All thy tediousness on me, ah?

DOGBERRY Yea, an't 'twere a thousand pound more than 'tis, for I hear as good exclamation on your worship as of any man in the city; and though I be but a poor man, I am glad to hear it.

VERGES And so am I.

LEONATO I would fain know what you have to say.

VERGES Marry, sir, our watch tonight, excepting your worship's presence, ha' ta'en a couple of as arrant knaves 30 as any in Messina.

DOGBERRY A good old man, sir, he will be talking; as they say, 'When the age is in, the wit is out.' God help us, it is a world to see! Well said, i'faith, neighbour Verges; well, God's a good man; an two men ride of a horse, one must ride behind. An honest soul, i'faith, sir, by my troth he is, as ever broke bread. But God is to be worshipped; all men are not alike. Alas, good neighbour!

LEONATO Indeed, neighbour, he comes too short of you.

40 DOGBERRY Gifts that God gives.

LEONATO I must leave you.

DOGBERRY One word, sir: our watch, sir, have indeed comprehended two aspicious persons, and we would have them this morning examined before your worship.

LEONATO Take their examination yourself and bring it me; I am now in great haste, as it may appear unto you.

DOGBERRY It shall be suffigance.

LEONATO Drink some wine ere you go. Fare you well.

Enter a Messenger

MESSENGER My lord, they stay for you to give your
50 daughter to her husband.

LEONATO I'll wait upon them; I am ready.

Exeunt Leonato and Messenger

DOGBERRY Go, good partner, go, get you to Francis Seacoal; bid him bring his pen and inkhorn to the gaol. We are now to examination these men.

VERGES And we must do it wisely.

DOGBERRY We will spare for no wit, I warrant you. Here's that shall drive some of them to a non-come; only get the learned writer to set down our excommunication, and meet me at the gaol.   *Exeunt*

*

IV.1   *Enter Don Pedro, Don John, Leonato, Friar Francis,*
               Claudio, Benedick, Hero, Beatrice, and attendants

LEONATO Come, Friar Francis, be brief; only to the plain form of marriage, and you shall recount their particular duties afterwards.

FRIAR You come hither, my lord, to marry this lady?

CLAUDIO No.

LEONATO To be married to her; Friar, you come to marry
  her!

FRIAR Lady, you come hither to be married to this Count?

HERO I do.

FRIAR If either of you know any inward impediment why 10
  you should not be conjoined, I charge you, on your souls,
  to utter it.

CLAUDIO Know you any, Hero?

HERO None, my lord.

FRIAR Know you any, Count?

LEONATO I dare make his answer, None.

CLAUDIO O, what men dare do! What men may do!
  What men daily do, not knowing what they do!

BENEDICK How now! Interjections? Why, then, some be
  of laughing, as, ah, ha, he! 20

CLAUDIO
Stand thee by, Friar. Father, by your leave:
Will you with free and unconstrainèd soul
Give me this maid, your daughter?

LEONATO
As freely, son, as God did give her me.

CLAUDIO
And what have I to give you back, whose worth
May counterpoise this rich and precious gift?

DON PEDRO
Nothing, unless you render her again.

CLAUDIO
Sweet Prince, you learn me noble thankfulness.
There, Leonato, take her back again,
Give not this rotten orange to your friend; 30
She's but the sign and semblance of her honour.
Behold how like a maid she blushes here!
O, what authority and show of truth
Can cunning sin cover itself withal!

Comes not that blood as modest evidence
To witness simple virtue? Would you not swear,
All you that see her, that she were a maid
By these exterior shows? But she is none;
She knows the heat of a luxurious bed.
40   Her blush is guiltiness, not modesty. ☆

LEONATO
What do you mean, my lord?

CLAUDIO   Not to be married,
Not to knit my soul to an approvèd wanton.

LEONATO
Dear my lord, if you, in your own proof,
Have vanquished the resistance of her youth,
And made defeat of her virginity –

CLAUDIO
I know what you would say. If I have known her,
You will say she did embrace me as a husband,
And so extenuate the 'forehand sin.
No, Leonato,
50   I never tempted her with word too large,
But, as a brother to his sister, showed
Bashful sincerity and comely love.

HERO
And seemed I ever otherwise to you?

CLAUDIO
Out on thee! Seeming! I will write against it.
You seem to me as Dian in her orb,
As chaste as is the bud ere it be blown;
But you are more intemperate in your blood
Than Venus, or those pampered animals
That rage in savage sensuality.

HERO
60   Is my lord well, that he doth speak so wide?

LEONATO
Sweet Prince, why speak not you?

DON PEDRO   What should I speak?
  I stand dishonoured, that have gone about
  To link my dear friend to a common stale.

LEONATO
  Are these things spoken, or do I but dream?

DON JOHN
  Sir, they are spoken, and these things are true.

BENEDICK
  This looks not like a nuptial.

HERO   True? O God!

CLAUDIO
  Leonato, stand I here?
  Is this the Prince? Is this the Prince's brother?
  Is this face Hero's? Are our eyes our own?

LEONATO
  All this is so; but what of this, my lord?   70

CLAUDIO
  Let me but move one question to your daughter;
  And, by that fatherly and kindly power
  That you have in her, bid her answer truly.

LEONATO
  I charge thee do so, as thou art my child.

HERO
  O God defend me! How am I beset!
  What kind of catechizing call you this?

CLAUDIO
  To make you answer truly to your name.

HERO
  Is it not Hero? Who can blot that name
  With any just reproach?

CLAUDIO   Marry, that can Hero;
  Hero itself can blot out Hero's virtue.   80
  What man was he talked with you yesternight
  Out at your window betwixt twelve and one?
  Now, if you are a maid, answer to this.

HERO

I talked with no man at that hour, my lord.

DON PEDRO

Why, then are you no maiden. Leonato,
I am sorry you must hear. Upon mine honour,
Myself, my brother, and this grievèd Count
Did see her, hear her, at that hour last night
Talk with a ruffian at her chamber-window;
90 Who hath, indeed, most like a liberal villain,
Confessed the vile encounters they have had
A thousand times in secret.

DON JOHN

Fie, fie, they are not to be named, my lord,
Not to be spoke of!
There is not chastity enough in language
Without offence to utter them. Thus, pretty lady,
I am sorry for thy much misgovernment.

CLAUDIO

O Hero! What a Hero hadst thou been,
If half thy outward graces had been placed
100 About thy thoughts and counsels of thy heart!
But fare thee well, most foul, most fair! Farewell,
Thou pure impiety and impious purity!
For thee I'll lock up all the gates of love,
And on my eyelids shall conjecture hang,
To turn all beauty into thoughts of harm,
And never shall it more be gracious.

LEONATO

Hath no man's dagger here a point for me?

Hero swoons

BEATRICE

Why, how now, cousin! Wherefore sink you down?

DON JOHN

Come, let us go. These things, come thus to light,

Smother her spirits up.
        Exeunt Don Pedro, Don John, and Claudio

BENEDICK
  How doth the lady?

BEATRICE   Dead, I think. Help, uncle!
  Hero! Why, Hero! Uncle! Signor Benedick! Friar!

LEONATO
  O Fate! Take not away thy heavy hand.
  Death is the fairest cover for her shame
  That may be wished for.

BEATRICE   How now, cousin Hero?

FRIAR
  Have comfort, lady.

LEONATO
  Dost thou look up?

FRIAR   Yea, wherefore should she not?

LEONATO
  Wherefore! Why, doth not every earthly thing
  Cry shame upon her? Could she here deny
  The story that is printed in her blood?   120
  Do not live, Hero, do not ope thine eyes;
  For, did I think thou wouldst not quickly die,
  Thought I thy spirits were stronger than thy shames,
  Myself would, on the rearward of reproaches,
  Strike at thy life. Grieved I, I had but one?
  Chid I for that at frugal Nature's frame?
  O, one too much by thee! Why had I one?
  Why ever wast thou lovely in my eyes?
  Why had I not with charitable hand
  Took up a beggar's issue at my gates,   130
  Who smirchèd thus and mired with infamy,
  I might have said 'No part of it is mine;
  This shame derives itself from unknown loins'?
  But mine and mine I loved and mine I praised

And mine that I was proud on, mine so much
That I myself was to myself not mine,
Valuing of her – why, she, O, she is fallen
Into a pit of ink, that the wide sea
Hath drops too few to wash her clean again
140 And salt too little which may season give
To her foul tainted flesh!

BENEDICK   Sir, sir, be patient.
For my part, I am so attired in wonder,
I know not what to say.

BEATRICE
O, on my soul, my cousin is belied!

BENEDICK
Lady, were you her bedfellow last night?

BEATRICE
No, truly not; although, until last night,
I have this twelvemonth been her bedfellow.

LEONATO
Confirmed, confirmed! O, that is stronger made
Which was before barred up with ribs of iron!
150 Would the two Princes lie, and Claudio lie,
Who loved her so, that, speaking of her foulness,
Washed it with tears? Hence from her, let her die!

FRIAR
Hear me a little;
For I have only silent been so long,
And given way unto this course of fortune
By noting of the lady. I have marked
A thousand blushing apparitions
To start into her face, a thousand innocent shames
In angel whiteness beat away those blushes;
160 And in her eye there hath appeared a fire,
To burn the errors that these Princes hold
Against her maiden truth. Call me a fool;

94

Trust not my reading nor my observations,
Which with experimental seal doth warrant
The tenor of my book; trust not my age,
My reverence, calling, nor divinity,
If this sweet lady lie not guiltless here
Under some biting error.

LEONATO   Friar, it cannot be.
Thou seest that all the grace that she hath left
Is that she will not add to her damnation   170
A sin of perjury; she not denies it:
Why seek'st thou then to cover with excuse
That which appears in proper nakedness?

FRIAR
Lady, what man is he you are accused of?

HERO
They know that do accuse me; I know none.
If I know more of any man alive
Than that which maiden modesty doth warrant,
Let all my sins lack mercy! O my father,
Prove you that any man with me conversed
At hours unmeet, or that I yesternight   180
Maintained the change of words with any creature,
Refuse me, hate me, torture me to death!

FRIAR
There is some strange misprision in the Princes.

BENEDICK
Two of them have the very bent of honour;
And if their wisdoms be misled in this,
The practice of it lives in John the Bastard,
Whose spirits toil in frame of villainies.

LEONATO
I know not. If they speak but truth of her,
These hands shall tear her; if they wrong her honour,
The proudest of them shall well hear of it.   190
Time hath not yet so dried this blood of mine,

95

Nor age so eat up my invention,
Nor fortune made such havoc of my means,
Nor my bad life reft me so much of friends,
But they shall find, awaked in such a kind,
Both strength of limb and policy of mind,
Ability in means and choice of friends
To quit me of them throughly.

FRIAR   Pause awhile,
And let my counsel sway you in this case.
200   Your daughter here the Princes left for dead;
Let her awhile be secretly kept in,
And publish it that she is dead indeed.
Maintain a mourning ostentation,
And on your family's old monument
Hang mournful epitaphs and do all rites
That appertain unto a burial.

LEONATO
What shall become of this? What will this do?

FRIAR
Marry, this, well carried, shall on her behalf
Change slander to remorse; that is some good.
210   But not for that dream I on this strange course,
But on this travail look for greater birth.
She dying, as it must be so maintained,
Upon the instant that she was accused,
Shall be lamented, pitied, and excused
Of every hearer; for it so falls out
That what we have we prize not to the worth
Whiles we enjoy it, but being lacked and lost,
Why, then we rack the value, then we find
The virtue that possession would not show us
220   Whiles it was ours. So will it fare with Claudio.
When he shall hear she died upon his words,
Th'idea of her life shall sweetly creep
Into his study of imagination,

compare with 96
Leonatos speech pg 93-94

And every lovely organ of her life
Shall come apparelled in more precious habit,
More moving, delicate, and full of life,
Into the eye and prospect of his soul,
Than when she lived indeed. Then shall he mourn,
If ever love had interest in his liver,
And wish he had not so accusèd her –   230
No, though he thought his accusation true.
Let this be so, and doubt not but success
Will fashion the event in better shape
Than I can lay it down in likelihood.
But if all aim but this be levelled false,
The supposition of the lady's death
Will quench the wonder of her infamy;
And if it sort not well, you may conceal her,
As best befits her wounded reputation,
In some reclusive and religious life,   240
Out of all eyes, tongues, minds, and injuries.

BENEDICK
Signor Leonato, let the Friar advise you;
And though you know my inwardness and love
Is very much unto the Prince and Claudio,
Yet, by mine honour, I will deal in this
As secretly and justly as your soul
Should with your body.

LEONATO   Being that I flow in grief,
The smallest twine may lead me.

FRIAR
'Tis well consented. Presently away;
For to strange sores strangely they strain the cure.   250
Come, lady, die to live; this wedding-day
Perhaps is but prolonged; have patience and endure.
              Exeunt all but Benedick and Beatrice

BENEDICK Lady Beatrice, have you wept all this while?
BEATRICE Yea, and I will weep a while longer.

97

BENEDICK I will not desire that.

BEATRICE You have no reason; I do it freely.

BENEDICK Surely I do believe your fair cousin is wronged.

BEATRICE Ah, how much might the man deserve of me that would right her!

260 BENEDICK Is there any way to show such friendship?

BEATRICE A very even way, but no such friend.

BENEDICK May a man do it?

BEATRICE It is a man's office, but not yours.

BENEDICK I do love nothing in the world so well as you; is not that strange?

BEATRICE As strange as the thing I know not. It were as possible for me to say I loved nothing so well as you; but believe me not, and yet I lie not; I confess nothing, nor I deny nothing. I am sorry for my cousin.

270 BENEDICK By my sword, Beatrice, thou lovest me.

BEATRICE Do not swear, and eat it.

BENEDICK I will swear by it that you love me; and I will make him eat it that says I love not you.

BEATRICE Will you not eat your word?

BENEDICK With no sauce that can be devised to it; I protest I love thee.

BEATRICE Why, then, God forgive me!

BENEDICK What offence, sweet Beatrice?

BEATRICE You have stayed me in a happy hour; I was
280 about to protest I loved you.

BENEDICK And do it with all thy heart.

BEATRICE I love you with so much of my heart that none is left to protest.

BENEDICK Come, bid me do anything for thee.

BEATRICE Kill Claudio.

BENEDICK Ha! Not for the wide world.

BEATRICE You kill me to deny it. Farewell.

BENEDICK (*taking her by the hand*) Tarry, sweet Beatrice.

BEATRICE I am gone though I am here; there is no love in you. Nay, I pray you, let me go. 290

BENEDICK Beatrice –

BEATRICE In faith, I will go.

BENEDICK We'll be friends first.

BEATRICE You dare easier be friends with me than fight with mine enemy.

BENEDICK Is Claudio thine enemy?

BEATRICE Is he not approved in the height a villain that hath slandered, scorned, dishonoured my kinswoman? O that I were a man! What, bear her in hand until they come to take hands, and then, with public accusation, 300 uncovered slander, unmitigated rancour – O God, that I were a man! I would eat his heart in the market-place.

BENEDICK Hear me, Beatrice –

BEATRICE Talk with a man out at a window! A proper saying!

BENEDICK Nay, but Beatrice –

BEATRICE Sweet Hero! She is wronged, she is slandered, she is undone.

BENEDICK Beat –

BEATRICE Princes and counties! Surely, a princely testi- 310 mony, a goodly count, Count Comfect; a sweet gallant, surely! O that I were a man for his sake, or that I had any friend would be a man for my sake! But manhood is melted into curtsies, valour into compliment, and men are only turned into tongue, and trim ones too. He is now as valiant as Hercules that only tells a lie and swears it. I cannot be a man with wishing, therefore I will die a woman with grieving.

BENEDICK Tarry, good Beatrice. By this hand, I love thee. 320

BEATRICE Use it for my love some other way than swearing by it.

99

BENEDICK Think you in your soul the Count Claudio hath
   wronged Hero?

BEATRICE Yea, as sure as I have a thought or a soul.

BENEDICK Enough, I am engaged; I will challenge him.
   I will kiss your hand, and so I leave you. By this hand,
   Claudio shall render me a dear account. As you hear of
   me, so think of me. Go, comfort your cousin; I must say
330   she is dead; and so, farewell.   *Exeunt*

IV.2   *Enter Dogberry, Verges, and the Sexton in gowns;*
            and the Watch, with Conrade and Borachio

DOGBERRY Is our whole dissembly appeared?

VERGES O, a stool and a cushion for the Sexton.

SEXTON Which be the malefactors?

DOGBERRY Marry, that am I and my partner.

VERGES Nay, that's certain; we have the exhibition to
   examine.

SEXTON But which are the offenders that are to be examined? Let them come before Master Constable.

DOGBERRY Yea, marry, let them come before me. What is
10 your name, friend?

BORACHIO Borachio.

DOGBERRY Pray, write down, Borachio. Yours, sirrah?

CONRADE I am a gentleman, sir, and my name is
   Conrade.

DOGBERRY Write down Master Gentleman Conrade.
   Masters, do you serve God?

CONRADE *and* BORACHIO Yea, sir, we hope.

DOGBERRY Write down, that they hope they serve God –
   and write God first, for God defend but God should go
20 before such villains! Masters, it is proved already that
   you are little better than false knaves, and it will go near
   to be thought so shortly. How answer you for yourselves?

CONRADE Marry, sir, we say we are none.

DOGBERRY A marvellous witty fellow, I assure you; but I will go about with him. Come you hither, sirrah; a word in your ear. Sir, I say to you, it is thought you are false knaves.

BORACHIO Sir, I say to you we are none.

DOGBERRY Well, stand aside. 'Fore God, they are both in 30 a tale. Have you writ down that they are none?

SEXTON Master Constable, you go not the way to examine; you must call forth the watch that are their accusers.

DOGBERRY Yea, marry, that's the eftest way; let the watch come forth. Masters, I charge you in the Prince's name, accuse these men.

FIRST WATCHMAN This man said, sir, that Don John, the Prince's brother, was a villain.

DOGBERRY Write down Prince John a villain. Why, this is flat perjury, to call a Prince's brother villain. 40

BORACHIO Master Constable –

DOGBERRY Pray thee, fellow, peace; I do not like thy look, I promise thee.

SEXTON What heard you him say else?

SECOND WATCHMAN Marry, that he had received a thousand ducats of Don John for accusing the Lady Hero wrongfully.

DOGBERRY Flat burglary as ever was committed.

VERGES Yea, by mass, that it is.

SEXTON What else, fellow? 50

FIRST WATCHMAN And that Count Claudio did mean, upon his words, to disgrace Hero before the whole assembly, and not marry her.

DOGBERRY O villain! Thou wilt be condemned into ever-lasting redemption for this.

SEXTON What else?

SECOND WATCHMAN This is all.

SEXTON And this is more, masters, than you can deny.

Prince John is this morning secretly stolen away; Hero
60 was in this manner accused, in this very manner refused,
and upon the grief of this suddenly died. Master Constable, let these men be bound, and brought to Leonato's; I will go before and show him their examination.   *Exit*

DOGBERRY Come, let them be opinioned.

VERGES Let them be – in the hands.

CONRADE Off, coxcomb!

DOGBERRY God's my life, where's the Sexton? Let him
write down the Prince's officer coxcomb. Come, bind
70 them. Thou naughty varlet!

CONRADE Away! You are an ass, you are an ass.

DOGBERRY Dost thou not suspect my place? Dost thou
not suspect my years? O that he were here to write me
down an ass! But, masters, remember that I am an ass;
though it be not written down, yet forget not that I am
an ass. No, thou villain, thou art full of piety, as shall be
proved upon thee by good witness. I am a wise fellow,
and, which is more, an officer; and, which is more, a
householder; and, which is more, as pretty a piece of
80 flesh as any is in Messina; and one that knows the law,
go to; and a rich fellow enough, go to; and a fellow that
hath had losses; and one that hath two gowns and everything handsome about him. Bring him away. O that I
had been writ down an ass!   *Exeunt*

*

ANTONIO

If you go on thus, you will kill yourself;
And 'tis not wisdom thus to second grief
Against yourself.

LEONATO   I pray thee, cease thy counsel,
Which falls into mine ears as profitless
As water in a sieve. Give not me counsel,
Nor let no comforter delight mine ear
But such a one whose wrongs do suit with mine.
Bring me a father that so loved his child,
Whose joy of her is overwhelmed like mine,
And bid him speak of patience;   10
Measure his woe the length and breadth of mine,
And let it answer every strain for strain,
And thus for thus, and such a grief for such,
In every lineament, branch, shape, and form;
If such a one will smile and stroke his beard,
And, sorry wag, cry 'hem!' when he should groan,
Patch grief with proverbs, make misfortune drunk
With candle-wasters – bring him yet to me,
And I of him will gather patience.
But there is no such man; for, brother, men   20
Can counsel and speak comfort to that grief
Which they themselves not feel; but, tasting it,
Their counsel turns to passion, which before
Would give preceptial medicine to rage,
Fetter strong madness in a silken thread,
Charm ache with air and agony with words.
No, no; 'tis all men's office to speak patience
To those that wring under the load of sorrow,
But no man's virtue nor sufficiency
To be so moral when he shall endure   30
The like himself. Therefore give me no counsel;

My griefs cry louder than advertisement.

ANTONIO

Therein do men from children nothing differ.

LEONATO

I pray thee, peace. I will be flesh and blood;
For there was never yet philosopher
That could endure the toothache patiently,
However they have writ the style of gods,
And made a push at chance and sufferance.

ANTONIO

Yet bend not all the harm upon yourself;
40   Make those that do offend you suffer too.

LEONATO

There thou speak'st reason; nay, I will do so.
My soul doth tell me Hero is belied,
And that shall Claudio know; so shall the Prince,
And all of them that thus dishonour her.

ANTONIO

Here comes the Prince and Claudio hastily.

Enter Don Pedro and Claudio

DON PEDRO

Good-e'en, good-e'en.

CLAUDIO   Good day to both of you.

LEONATO

Hear you, my lords!

DON PEDRO   We have some haste, Leonato.

LEONATO

Some haste, my lord! Well, fare you well, my lord;
Are you so hasty now? Well, all is one.

DON PEDRO

50   Nay, do not quarrel with us, good old man.

ANTONIO

If he could right himself with quarrelling,
Some of us would lie low.

CLAUDIO   Who wrongs him?

LEONATO

Marry, thou dost wrong me, thou dissembler, thou!
– Nay, never lay thy hand upon thy sword;
I fear thee not.

CLAUDIO   Marry, beshrew my hand,
If it should give your age such cause of fear:
In faith, my hand meant nothing to my sword.

LEONATO

Tush, tush, man, never fleer and jest at me;
I speak not like a dotard nor a fool,
As under privilege of age to brag   60
What I have done being young, or what would do
Were I not old. Know, Claudio, to thy head,
Thou hast so wronged mine innocent child and me
That I am forced to lay my reverence by,
And with grey hairs and bruise of many days,
Do challenge thee to trial of a man.
I say thou hast belied mine innocent child.
Thy slander hath gone through and through her heart,
And she lies buried with her ancestors –
O, in a tomb where never scandal slept,   70
Save this of hers, framed by thy villainy!

CLAUDIO

My villainy?

LEONATO   Thine, Claudio; thine, I say.

DON PEDRO

You say not right, old man.

LEONATO   My lord, my lord,
I'll prove it on his body if he dare,
Despite his nice fence and his active practice,
His May of youth and bloom of lustihood.

CLAUDIO

Away! I will not have to do with you.

LEONATO

Canst thou so daff me? Thou hast killed my child;
If thou kill'st me, boy, thou shalt kill a man.

ANTONIO

80 He shall kill two of us, and men indeed;
But that's no matter, let him kill one first.
Win me and wear me; let him answer me.
Come, follow me, boy; come, sir boy, come, follow me;
Sir boy, I'll whip you from your foining fence;
Nay, as I am a gentleman, I will.

LEONATO

Brother –

ANTONIO

Content yourself. God knows I loved my niece;
And she is dead, slandered to death by villains,
That dare as well answer a man indeed
90 As I dare take a serpent by the tongue.
Boys, apes, braggarts, Jacks, milksops!

LEONATO   Brother Antony –

ANTONIO

Hold you content. What, man! I know them, yea,
And what they weigh, even to the utmost scruple –
Scambling, out-facing, fashion-monging boys,
That lie and cog and flout, deprave and slander,
Go anticly, show outward hideousness,
And speak off half a dozen dangerous words,
How they might hurt their enemies, if they durst;
And this is all.

LEONATO

100 But, brother Antony –

ANTONIO   Come, 'tis no matter;
Do not you meddle, let me deal in this.

DON PEDRO

Gentlemen both, we will not wake your patience.

My heart is sorry for your daughter's death,
But, on my honour, she was charged with nothing
But what was true and very full of proof.

LEONATO
My lord, my lord –
DON PEDRO   I will not hear you.
LEONATO   No?
Come brother, away. I will be heard.

ANTONIO
And shall, or some of us will smart for it.

Exeunt Leonato and Antonio

DON PEDRO
See, see; here comes the man we went to seek.

Enter Benedick

CLAUDIO Now, signor, what news?   110

BENEDICK Good day, my lord.

DON PEDRO Welcome, signor; you are almost come to part almost a fray.

CLAUDIO We had like to have had our two noses snapped off with two old men without teeth.

DON PEDRO Leonato and his brother. What think'st thou? Had we fought, I doubt we should have been too young for them.

BENEDICK In a false quarrel there is no true valour. I came to seek you both.   120

CLAUDIO We have been up and down to seek thee, for we are high-proof melancholy, and would fain have it beaten away. Wilt thou use thy wit?

BENEDICK It is in my scabbard; shall I draw it?

DON PEDRO Dost thou wear thy wit by thy side?

CLAUDIO Never any did so, though very many have been beside their wit. I will bid thee draw, as we do the minstrels – draw to pleasure us.

DON PEDRO As I am an honest man, he looks pale.

107

130   Art thou sick, or angry?

CLAUDIO What, courage, man! What though care killed
a cat, thou hast mettle enough in thee to kill care.

BENEDICK Sir, I shall meet your wit in the career, an you
charge it against me. I pray you choose another subject.

CLAUDIO Nay, then, give him another staff; this last was
broke cross.

DON PEDRO By this light, he changes more and more; I
think he be angry indeed.

CLAUDIO If he be, he knows how to turn his girdle.

140 BENEDICK Shall I speak a word in your ear?

CLAUDIO God bless me from a challenge!

BENEDICK (*aside to Claudio*) You are a villain; I jest not.
I will make it good how you dare, with what you dare,
and when you dare. Do me right, or I will protest your
cowardice. You have killed a sweet lady, and her death
shall fall heavy on you. Let me hear from you.

CLAUDIO Well, I will meet you, so I may have good cheer.

DON PEDRO What, a feast, a feast?

CLAUDIO I'faith, I thank him; he hath bid me to a calf's
150 head and a capon, the which if I do not carve most
curiously, say my knife's naught. Shall I not find a
woodcock too?

BENEDICK Sir, your wit ambles well; it goes easily.

DON PEDRO I'll tell thee how Beatrice praised thy wit the
other day. I said, thou hadst a fine wit. 'True,' said she,
'a fine little one.' 'No,' said I, 'a great wit.' 'Right,' says
she, 'a great gross one.' 'Nay,' said I, 'a good wit.' 'Just,'
said she, 'it hurts nobody.' 'Nay,' said I, 'the gentleman
is wise.' 'Certain,' said she, 'a wise gentleman.' 'Nay,'
160 said I, 'he hath the tongues.' 'That I believe,' said she,
'for he swore a thing to me on Monday night, which he
forswore on Tuesday morning. There's a double
tongue: there's two tongues.' Thus did she, an hour

together, trans-shape thy particular virtues; yet at last
she concluded with a sigh, thou wast the properest man
in Italy.

CLAUDIO For the which she wept heartily, and said she
cared not.

DON PEDRO Yea, that she did; but yet, for all that, an if
she did not hate him deadly, she would love him dearly. 170
The old man's daughter told us all.

CLAUDIO All, all; and, moreover, God saw him when he
was hid in the garden.

DON PEDRO But when shall we set the savage bull's
horns on the sensible Benedick's head?

CLAUDIO Yes, and text underneath, 'Here dwells Benedick, the married man'?

BENEDICK Fare you well, boy; you know my mind. I will
leave you now to your gossip-like humour; you break
jests as braggarts do their blades, which, God be 180
thanked, hurt not. (*To Don Pedro*) My lord, for your
many courtesies I thank you; I must discontinue your
company. Your brother the Bastard is fled from
Messina. You have among you killed a sweet and innocent lady. For my Lord Lackbeard there, he and I shall
meet; and till then, peace be with him.   *Exit*

DON PEDRO He is in earnest.

CLAUDIO In most profound earnest; and, I'll warrant
you, for the love of Beatrice.

DON PEDRO And hath challenged thee.   190

CLAUDIO Most sincerely.

DON PEDRO What a pretty thing man is when he goes in
his doublet and hose and leaves off his wit!

CLAUDIO He is then a giant to an ape; but then is an ape
a doctor to such a man.

DON PEDRO But, soft you, let me be; pluck up, my heart,
and be sad. Did he not say, my brother was fled?

Enter Dogberry, Verges, Watch, Conrade, and
Borachio

DOGBERRY Come, you, sir; if justice cannot tame you, she
shall ne'er weigh more reasons in her balance. Nay, an
200   you be a cursing hypocrite once, you must be looked to.

DON PEDRO How now, two of my brother's men bound?
Borachio one!

CLAUDIO Hearken after their offence, my lord.

DON PEDRO Officers, what offence have these men done?

DOGBERRY Marry, sir, they have committed false report;
moreover they have spoken untruths; secondarily, they
are slanders; sixth and lastly, they have belied a lady;
thirdly, they have verified unjust things; and, to conclude, they are lying knaves.

210 DON PEDRO First, I ask thee what they have done; thirdly,
I ask thee what's their offence; sixth and lastly, why
they are committed; and, to conclude, what you lay to
their charge.

CLAUDIO Rightly reasoned, and in his own division; and,
by my troth, there's one meaning well suited.

DON PEDRO Who have you offended, masters, that you
are thus bound to your answer? This learned Constable
is too cunning to be understood; what's your offence?

BORACHIO Sweet Prince, let me go no farther to mine
220   answer; do you hear me, and let this Count kill me. I
have deceived even your very eyes: what your wisdoms
could not discover, these shallow fools have brought to
light; who in the night overheard me confessing to this
man how Don John your brother incensed me to slander
the Lady Hero; how you were brought into the orchard
and saw me court Margaret in Hero's garments; how
you disgraced her, when you should marry her. My villainy they have upon record, which I had rather seal
with my death than repeat over to my shame. The lady

is dead upon mine and my master's false accusation; and, 230
briefly, I desire nothing but the reward of a villain.

DON PEDRO
Runs not this speech like iron through your blood?

CLAUDIO
I have drunk poison whiles he uttered it.

DON PEDRO
But did my brother set thee on to this?

BORACHIO
Yes, and paid me richly for the practice of it.

DON PEDRO
He is composed and framed of treachery,
And fled he is upon this villainy.

CLAUDIO
Sweet Hero, now thy image doth appear
In the rare semblance that I loved it first.

DOGBERRY Come, bring away the plaintiffs; by this time 240
our Sexton hath reformed Signor Leonato of the matter.
And, masters, do not forget to specify, when time and
place shall serve, that I am an ass.

VERGES Here, here comes master Signor Leonato, and
the Sexton too.

Enter Leonato and Antonio, with the Sexton

LEONATO
Which is the villain? Let me see his eyes,
That, when I note another man like him,
I may avoid him. Which of these is he?

BORACHIO
If you would know your wronger, look on me.

LEONATO
Art thou the slave that with thy breath hast killed 250
Mine innocent child?

BORACHIO   Yea, even I alone.

LEONATO

No, not so, villain, thou beliest thyself –
Here stand a pair of honourable men,
A third is fled, that had a hand in it.
I thank you, Princes, for my daughter's death;
Record it with your high and worthy deeds.
'Twas bravely done, if you bethink you of it.

CLAUDIO

I know not how to pray your patience,
Yet I must speak. Choose your revenge yourself;
260   Impose me to what penance your invention
Can lay upon my sin; yet sinned I not
But in mistaking.

DON PEDRO   By my soul, nor I;

And yet, to satisfy this good old man,
I would bend under any heavy weight
That he'll enjoin me to.

LEONATO

I cannot bid you bid my daughter live,
That were impossible; but, I pray you both,
Possess the people in Messina here
How innocent she died; and if your love
270   Can labour aught in sad invention,
Hang her an epitaph upon her tomb
And sing it to her bones, sing it tonight.
Tomorrow morning come you to my house;
And since you could not be my son-in-law,
Be yet my nephew. My brother hath a daughter,
Almost the copy of my child that's dead,
And she alone is heir to both of us.
Give her the right you should have given her cousin,
And so dies my revenge.

CLAUDIO   O noble sir!

280   Your over-kindness doth wring tears from me.

I do embrace your offer, and dispose
For henceforth of poor Claudio.

LEONATO
Tomorrow then I will expect your coming;
Tonight I take my leave. This naughty man
Shall face to face be brought to Margaret,
Who I believe was packed in all this wrong,
Hired to it by your brother.

BORACHIO   No, by my soul, she was not,
Nor knew not what she did when she spoke to me,
But always hath been just and virtuous
In anything that I do know by her.   290

DOGBERRY Moreover, sir, which indeed is not under
white and black, this plaintiff here, the offender, did call
me ass; I beseech you, let it be remembered in his
punishment. And also, the watch heard them talk of one
Deformed; they say he wears a key in his ear and a lock
hanging by it, and borrows money in God's name, the
which he hath used so long and never paid, that now
men grow hard-hearted and will lend nothing for God's
sake. Pray you, examine him upon that point.

LEONATO
I thank thee for thy care and honest pains.   300

DOGBERRY Your worship speaks like a most thankful and
reverend youth, and I praise God for you.

LEONATO There's for thy pains.

DOGBERRY God save the foundation!

LEONATO Go, I discharge thee of thy prisoner, and I
thank thee.

DOGBERRY I leave an arrant knave with your worship;
which I beseech your worship to correct yourself, for the
example of others. God keep your worship! I wish your
worship well; God restore you to health! I humbly give   310
you leave to depart; and if a merry meeting may be

wished, God prohibit it! Come, neighbour.

Exeunt Dogberry and Verges

LEONATO
Until tomorrow morning, lords, farewell.

ANTONIO
Farewell, my lords; we look for you tomorrow.

DON PEDRO
We will not fail.

CLAUDIO   Tonight I'll mourn with Hero.

Exeunt Don Pedro and Claudio

LEONATO (*to the Watch*)
Bring you these fellows on. We'll talk with Margaret,
How her acquaintance grew with this lewd fellow.

Exeunt

V.2   *Enter Benedick and Margaret*

BENEDICK Pray thee, sweet Mistress Margaret, deserve
well at my hands by helping me to the speech of
Beatrice.

MARGARET Will you then write me a sonnet in praise of
my beauty?

BENEDICK In so high a style, Margaret, that no man living shall come over it; for, in most comely truth, thou
deservest it.

MARGARET To have no man come over me! Why, shall I
10 always keep below stairs?

BENEDICK Thy wit is as quick as the greyhound's mouth;
it catches.

MARGARET And yours as blunt as the fencer's foils, which
hit, but hurt not.

BENEDICK A most manly wit, Margaret; it will not hurt a
woman. And so, I pray thee, call Beatrice; I give thee
the bucklers.

MARGARET Give us the swords; we have bucklers of our own.

BENEDICK If you use them, Margaret, you must put in 20 the pikes with a vice; and they are dangerous weapons for maids.

MARGARET Well, I will call Beatrice to you, who I think hath legs.   *Exit Margaret*

BENEDICK And therefore will come.

(*sings*) The God of love,
            That sits above,
            And knows me, and knows me,
            How pitiful I deserve –

I mean in singing; but in loving, Leander the good 30 swimmer, Troilus the first employer of panders, and a whole bookful of these quondam carpet-mongers, whose names yet run smoothly in the even road of a blank verse, why, they were never so truly turned over and over as my poor self in love. Marry, I cannot show it in rhyme, I have tried; I can find out no rhyme to 'lady' but 'baby' – an innocent rhyme; for 'scorn', 'horn' – a hard rhyme; for 'school', 'fool' – a babbling rhyme; very ominous endings. No, I was not born under a rhyming planet, nor I cannot woo in festival terms. 40

Enter Beatrice

Sweet Beatrice, wouldst thou come when I called thee?

BEATRICE Yea, signor, and depart when you bid me.

BENEDICK O, stay but till then!

BEATRICE 'Then' is spoken; fare you well now. And yet, ere I go, let me go with that I came, which is, with knowing what hath passed between you and Claudio.

BENEDICK Only foul words; and thereupon I will kiss thee.

BEATRICE Foul words is but foul wind, and foul wind is but foul breath, and foul breath is noisome; therefore I will depart unkissed.   50

BENEDICK Thou hast frighted the word out of his right sense, so forcible is thy wit. But I must tell thee plainly, Claudio undergoes my challenge; and either I must shortly hear from him, or I will subscribe him a coward. And I pray thee now, tell me for which of my bad parts didst thou first fall in love with me?

BEATRICE For them all together; which maintained so politic a state of evil that they will not admit any good part to intermingle with them. But for which of my good
60 parts did you first suffer love for me?

BENEDICK Suffer love! A good epithet, I do suffer love indeed, for I love thee against my will.

BEATRICE In spite of your heart, I think; alas, poor heart! If you spite it for my sake, I will spite it for yours; for I will never love that which my friend hates.

BENEDICK Thou and I are too wise to woo peaceably.

BEATRICE It appears not in this confession; there's not one wise man among twenty that will praise himself.

BENEDICK An old, an old instance, Beatrice, that lived in
70 the time of good neighbours. If a man do not erect in this age his own tomb ere he dies, he shall live no longer in monument than the bell rings and the widow weeps.

BEATRICE And how long is that, think you?

BENEDICK Question – why, an hour in clamour and a quarter in rheum. Therefore is it most expedient for the wise, if Don Worm, his conscience, find no impediment to the contrary, to be the trumpet of his own virtues, as I am to myself. So much for praising myself, who, I myself will bear witness, is praiseworthy. And now tell
80 me, how doth your cousin?

BEATRICE Very ill.

BENEDICK And how do you?

BEATRICE Very ill too.

BENEDICK Serve God, love me, and mend. There will I leave you too, for here comes one in haste.

Enter Ursula

URSULA Madam, you must come to your uncle. Yonder's
old coil at home; it is proved my Lady Hero hath been
falsely accused, the Prince and Claudio mightily abused,
and Don John is the author of all, who is fled and gone.
Will you come presently?   90

BEATRICE Will you go hear this news, signor?

BENEDICK I will live in thy heart, die in thy lap and be
buried in thy eyes; and moreover, I will go with thee to
thy uncle's.   *Exeunt*

Enter Claudio, Don Pedro, Balthasar, and three or V.3
four with tapers, all wearing mourning

CLAUDIO Is this the monument of Leonato?

A LORD It is, my lord.

CLAUDIO (*reading from a scroll*)

Epitaph

Done to death by slanderous tongues
    Was the Hero that here lies:
Death, in guerdon of her wrongs,
    Gives her fame which never dies.
So the life that died with shame
Lives in death with glorious fame.
    Hang thou there upon the tomb
    Praising her when I am dumb.   10

Now, music, sound, and sing your solemn hymn.

Song

BALTHASAR

    Pardon, goddess of the night,
    Those that slew thy virgin knight;
    For the which, with songs of woe,
    Round about her tomb they go.

> Midnight, assist our moan,
> Help us to sigh and groan,
>   Heavily, heavily.
> Graves yawn and yield your dead,
20   Till death be utterèd,
>   Heavily, heavily.

CLAUDIO

Now, unto thy bones good night!
Yearly will I do this rite.

DON PEDRO

Good morrow, masters; put your torches out;
   The wolves have preyed, and look, the gentle day,
Before the wheels of Phoebus, round about
   Dapples the drowsy east with spots of grey.
Thanks to you all, and leave us: fare you well.

CLAUDIO

   Good morrow, masters: each his several way.

DON PEDRO

30 Come, let us hence, and put on other weeds;
   And then to Leonato's we will go.

CLAUDIO

And Hymen now with luckier issue speed's
   Than this for whom we rendered up this woe. *Exeunt*

V.4   *Enter Leonato, Antonio, Benedick, Beatrice, Margaret, Ursula, Friar Francis, and Hero*

FRIAR

Did I not tell you she was innocent?

LEONATO

So are the Prince and Claudio, who accused her
Upon the error that you heard debated;
But Margaret was in some fault for this,
Although against her will, as it appears
In the true course of all the question.

ANTONIO

Well, I am glad that all things sort so well.

BENEDICK

And so am I, being else by faith enforced
To call young Claudio to a reckoning for it.

LEONATO

Well, daughter, and you gentlewomen all,   10
Withdraw into a chamber by yourselves,
And when I send for you, come hither masked.
The Prince and Claudio promised by this hour
To visit me. You know your office, brother;
You must be father to your brother's daughter,
And give her to young Claudio.   *Exeunt Ladies*

ANTONIO

Which I will do with confirmed countenance.

BENEDICK

Friar, I must entreat your pains, I think.

FRIAR

To do what, signor?

BENEDICK

To bind me, or undo me – one of them.   20
Signor Leonato, truth it is, good signor,
Your niece regards me with an eye of favour.

LEONATO

That eye my daughter lent her; 'tis most true.

BENEDICK

And I do with an eye of love requite her.

LEONATO

The sight whereof I think you had from me,
From Claudio, and the Prince; but what's your will?

BENEDICK

Your answer, sir, is enigmatical;
But, for my will, my will is your good will
May stand with ours, this day to be conjoined
In the state of honourable marriage –   30

In which, good Friar, I shall desire your help.

LEONATO

My heart is with your liking.

FRIAR   And my help.

Here comes the Prince and Claudio.

Enter Don Pedro and Claudio, and two or three others

DON PEDRO

Good morrow to this fair assembly.

LEONATO

Good morrow, Prince; good morrow, Claudio;

We here attend you. Are you yet determined

Today to marry with my brother's daughter?

CLAUDIO

I'll hold my mind, were she an Ethiope.

LEONATO

Call her forth, brother; here's the Friar ready.

Exit Antonio

DON PEDRO

40 Good morrow, Benedick. Why, what's the matter,

That you have such a February face,

So full of frost, of storm and cloudiness?

CLAUDIO

I think he thinks upon the savage bull.

Tush, fear not, man, we'll tip thy horns with gold,

And all Europa shall rejoice at thee,

As once Europa did at lusty Jove,

When he would play the noble beast in love.

BENEDICK

Bull Jove, sir, had an amiable low;

And some such strange bull leaped your father's cow,

50 And got a calf in that same noble feat

Much like to you, for you have just his bleat.

CLAUDIO

For this I owe you: here comes other reckonings.

Enter Antonio, with the Ladies masked
Which is the lady I must seize upon?

ANTONIO
This same is she, and I do give you her.

CLAUDIO
Why, then she's mine. Sweet, let me see your face.

ANTONIO
No, that you shall not, till you take her hand
Before this Friar and swear to marry her.

CLAUDIO
Give me your hand; before this holy Friar,
I am your husband, if you like of me.

HERO (*unmasking*)
And when I lived, I was your other wife;   60
And when you loved, you were my other husband.

CLAUDIO
Another Hero!

HERO   Nothing certainer;
One Hero died defiled, but I do live,
And surely as I live, I am a maid.

DON PEDRO
The former Hero! Hero that is dead!

LEONATO
She died, my lord, but whiles her slander lived.

FRIAR
All this amazement can I qualify,
When, after that the holy rites are ended,
I'll tell you largely of fair Hero's death.
Meantime let wonder seem familiar,   70
And to the chapel let us presently.

BENEDICK
Soft and fair, Friar. Which is Beatrice?

BEATRICE (*unmasking*)
I answer to that name. What is your will?

BENEDICK
Do not you love me?

BEATRICE   Why no, no more than reason.

BENEDICK
Why, then your uncle and the Prince and Claudio
Have been deceived; they swore you did.

BEATRICE
Do not you love me?

BENEDICK   Troth no, no more than reason.

BEATRICE
Why, then my cousin, Margaret, and Ursula
Are much deceived; for they did swear you did.

BENEDICK
80 They swore that you were almost sick for me.

BEATRICE
They swore that you were well-nigh dead for me.

BENEDICK
'Tis no such matter. Then you do not love me?

BEATRICE
No, truly, but in friendly recompense.

LEONATO
Come, cousin, I am sure you love the gentleman.

CLAUDIO
And I'll be sworn upon't that he loves her,
For here's a paper written in his hand,
A halting sonnet of his own pure brain,
Fashioned to Beatrice.

HERO   And here's another
Writ in my cousin's hand, stolen from her pocket,
90 Containing her affection unto Benedick.

BENEDICK A miracle! Here's our own hands against our
hearts. Come, I will have thee; but, by this light, I take
thee for pity.

BEATRICE I would not deny you; but, by this good day, I
yield upon great persuasion; and partly to save your

life, for I was told you were in a consumption.

BENEDICK (*kissing her*) Peace! I will stop your mouth.

DON PEDRO How dost thou, Benedick the married man?

BENEDICK I'll tell thee what, Prince; a college of wit-crackers cannot flout me out of my humour. Dost thou 100 think I care for a satire or an epigram? No; if a man will be beaten with brains, 'a shall wear nothing handsome about him. In brief, since I do purpose to marry, I will think nothing to any purpose that the world can say against it; and therefore never flout at me for what I have said against it; for man is a giddy thing, and this is my conclusion. For thy part, Claudio, I did think to have beaten thee; but in that thou art like to be my kins-man, live unbruised and love my cousin.

CLAUDIO I had well hoped thou wouldst have denied 110 Beatrice, that I might have cudgelled thee out of thy single life, to make thee a double-dealer; which out of question thou wilt be, if my cousin do not look exceed-ing narrowly to thee.

BENEDICK Come, come, we are friends. Let's have a dance ere we are married, that we may lighten our own hearts and our wives' heels.

LEONATO We'll have dancing afterward.

BENEDICK First, of my word; therefore play, music. Prince, thou art sad; get thee a wife, get thee a wife. 120 There is no staff more reverend than one tipped with horn.

Enter a Messenger

MESSENGER
My lord, your brother John is ta'en in flight,
And brought with armed men back to Messina.

BENEDICK Think not on him till tomorrow; I'll devise thee brave punishments for him. Strike up, pipers.

Dance, and then exeunt

COMMENTARY

THE Act and scene divisions are those of Peter Alexander's edition of the *Complete Works* (1951). All references to other plays by Shakespeare not yet available in the New Penguin Shakespeare are to Alexander.

In the Commentary and Account of the Text, the abbreviations Q and F refer respectively to the Quarto (1600), and first collected edition of Shakespeare's plays, the Folio of 1623. In quotations from these early editions the 'long s' (ſ) has been replaced by 's'.

The Title
Much Ado About Nothing exemplifies a kind of deliberately puzzling title that seems to have been popular in the late 1590s (compare *As You Like It*, or the plays staged by the rival company to Shakespeare's, the Lord Admiral's Men, under titles like *Crack Me this Nut*, and *Chance Medley*). The title *Much Ado About Nothing* has, of course, a direct meaning in relation to the play's main action, concerning Claudio and Hero, which proves in the end to be ado about nothing. It also contains a pun on the word 'noting', as illustrated by Don Pedro's remark on Balthasar at II.3.55, 'Note notes, forsooth, and nothing'; here the quibble is mainly on 'noting' as notation in a musical score. In the title, the sense 'observing' seems stronger, as the play is much concerned with people observing and overhearing one another, and making a great deal out of nothing. The implications have been fully worked out by P. A. Jorgensen in *Redeeming Shakespeare's Words* (1962). Matters of staging, and the passage of time, are dealt with in headnotes to individual scenes.

.1   (stage direction) *Messina.* The setting is taken from Bandello. King Peter of Aragon, ruler of Sicily, held

125

court in Messina after the Sicilian Vespers in 1283; he died in 1285. The action takes place at or outside the house of Leonato; on Shakespeare's stage this was probably suggested adequately by the stage façade. See Introduction, p. 23. Both Q and F list 'Innogen his wife' as entering after Leonato, but she has no part in the play.

(stage direction) *Hero.* She embodies faithfulness in love, as her name recalls the story of Hero and Leander; see also IV.1.80 and note, and V.2.30–31.

1, 9   *Pedro.* Q and F have 'Peter' here; for other anglicizations of names, see III.1, first stage direction and line 4, and V.1.91 (Antony).

6   *action* battle

7   *name* distinction

12–13   *equally remembered* justly rewarded

13–16   *He hath borne himself . . . tell you how.* The Messenger's manner is slightly pompous; his speech combines antithesis and alliteration, with an echo of Euphuism; see Introduction, p. 25.

17   *uncle.* The uncle does not appear in the play.

21   *modest* moderate

21–2   *badge of bitterness* tears. Their master's 'badge' or device was worn by servants on the sleeve, a mark of humble status, and so of modesty.

25   *kind* natural

28   *Mountanto* an upright thrust in fencing. Beatrice well knows Benedick as a (verbal) duellist with her.

31   *sort* rank

34   *pleasant* merry

36   *set up his bills* posted notices

37   *at the flight* to a shooting contest. Benedick claims to be a better archer than Cupid, that is, a lady-killer, and, as he says later, a 'tyrant to their sex' (lines 158–9).

38   *subscribed for* signed on behalf of

39   *bird-bolt* a blunt-headed arrow used for shooting birds; it was also the allowed weapon of the fool (compare the

proverb, 'A fool's bolt is soon shot'), as being fairly harmless. Benedick claimed expert skill in challenging Cupid; the fool implies that he is a novice by challenging him at the lowest level of archery.

42   *tax* disparage

43   *meet* even

46   *holp.* The early strong inflection only gradually gave way to the modern 'helped'; Shakespeare uses both forms.

47   *valiant trencher-man* hearty eater

50   *to* in comparison with

52   *stuffed* well-stored (a proper usage)

54   *stuffed man* (suggesting a figure stuffed to look like a man)

61   *five wits* (mental faculties, numbered five by vague analogy with the five senses, and sometimes named as common sense, imagination, fantasy, estimation, and memory)

        halting limping

63-4   *bear it for a difference* (in heraldry, to show 'an alteration of or an addition to a coat of arms, to distinguish a junior member or branch of a family from the chief line' – *Oxford English Dictionary*)

65-6   *reasonable creature.* This was a phrase applied to all living creatures, not just to human beings; Beatrice implies that Benedick is little better than his horse.

69   *faith* loyalty to his 'sworn brother'

71   *block* mould (and so shape or fashion)

72   *books* good books, favour

73, 178, 187 *an* if

75   *squarer* swaggerer

81   *presently* at once

84   *I will hold friends with you* I will take care not to cross you

86   *run mad* (catch the Benedick, and meaning also 'fall in love with him')

88   *is* has (a survival of an old usage with verbs of motion)

        (stage direction) *Bastard.* The first indication in the

text that Don John is a bastard comes at IV.1.186. His bastardy partly explains his temperament; Bacon says in his essay *Of Envy*, 'Bastards are envious: for he that cannot possibly mend his own case, will do what he can to impair others.'

90   *trouble* (the burden and expense of entertaining the Prince and his retinue)

96   *charge* expense, and responsibility

101   *have it full* are well answered

102-3   *fathers herself* shows who her father is by resembling him

106   *his head* (meaning his beard and grey or white hair)

113   *meet* proper (with a quibble on 'meat')

114   *convert* change

120   *dear happiness* precious piece of luck

122   *of your humour for that* of your frame of mind on that point

130   *rare parrot-teacher* fine chatterer. Like one teaching a parrot, she repeats herself and talks little sense, says Benedick.

131-2   *A bird of my tongue is better than a beast of yours* (a talking bird is better than a dumb beast)

134   *continuer* one having the power to keep going

136   *with a jade's trick* (by stopping suddenly, like an ill-tempered horse, and throwing me off)

138   *That is the sum of all, Leonato.* Don Pedro has been talking aside with Leonato, and now turns to include the others in his address.

140   *all* (including Don John and Balthasar)

146   *being* since you are

150   *Please it* may it please

154   *noted her not* did not give her special attention

161   *low* short

171   *sad* serious

    flouting Jack mocking knave. 'Jack' was used as a common noun, meaning 'fellow'; compare 'a swearing Jack', *The Taming of the Shrew*, II.1.281.

172-3   *Cupid is a good hare-finder . . . carpenter.* The joke is that

Cupid was blind, and good sight is needed to spot a hare; and Vulcan, god of fire, was a blacksmith.

173   *go* join

185   *wear his cap with suspicion* (get married, and be suspected of wearing a cap to hide his cuckold's horns)

188   *sigh away Sundays* (because on Sundays, or days of leisure, he will feel his bondage most sharply)

197   *who* whom (a common usage)
      part (to ask that question)

199   *If this were so, so were it uttered.* Claudio speaks evasively: 'If I had told him such a secret, he would have revealed it in this way.'

200   *old tale.* An old tale which contains the refrain quoted was reported in the 1821 Variorum edition of Shakespeare; its authenticity is doubtful, but it illustrates Benedick's meaning. In it a villain repeatedly denies his crimes when they are described to him, until at last proof is laid before him; so, however much Claudio denies that he is in love, the truth is evident.

206   *fetch me in* trick me into a confession

209   *two faiths and troths* (a joking allusion to the clash between his loyalty to Don Pedro, and his friendship to Claudio)

216–17 *in the despite of* in showing contempt for

218–19 *in the force of his will* by mere obstinacy (suggesting the wilfulness of the heretic in maintaining a false opinion)

222–3   *have a recheat ... invisible baldrick* have a call for assembling the hounds sounded in my forehead, or hang my hunting-horn in an invisible belt. In other words, Benedick will be neither an open nor an unacknowledged cuckold, will neither display nor conceal cuckold's horns – implying that one or other is the fate of all married men.

226   *fine* conclusion

230–31 *lose more blood with love ... drinking.* It was commonly believed that sighing dried up the blood, and that drinking wine produced new blood.

232   *ballad-maker's* (as ballads were mainly of love)

236   *argument* topic for conversation

237   *hang me in a bottle like a cat.* A cat suspended in a
       leather bottle or basket was used sometimes as a target
       for practice in archery.

239   *Adam* (after Adam Bell, a famous archer)

241   '*In time the savage bull doth bear the yoke*'. The line is
       roughly quoted from Thomas Kyd's *The Spanish Trag-
       edy* (about 1587), II.1.3, 'In time the savage bull sustains
       the yoke', where, in turn, it is borrowed from Sonnet
       47 of Thomas Watson's *Hecatompathia* (1582).

249   *horn-mad* furious (as bulls attack with horns when
       enraged – and with an allusion also to cuckolds' horns)

251   *Venice* (in Shakespeare's day, a city famous for its
       courtesans and sexual licence)

252   *earthquake* (meaning that it will take a huge convulsion
       to affect him)

253   *temporize with the hours* weaken as time goes by

258   *matter* sense

260   *tuition* care. Claudio parodies the formal ending of a
       letter.

265   *guarded* ornamented

266   *basted* loosely tacked on

266–7 *flout old ends* mock me with old tags (like the quotation
       at line 241 and the parody at lines 260–63). 'Old ends'
       suggest also the 'fragments' of cloth of the previous
       sentence.

269   *do me good* help me

275   *affect* care for

276   *ended action* war just ended

280   *now I* now that I

283   *prompting* reminding

286   *book of words* as every lover should pour out words,
       preferably rhymes, in praise of his mistress. Even
       Benedick tries his hand at it in V.2.

288   *break* broach the matter

292   *complexion* appearance (the lover looks pale)

294   *salved it* accounted for it (a sense once common)
         treatise narrative
296   *The fairest grant is the necessity* the best gift is what
         satisfies a need
         Look what whatever
         'Tis once once for all
302   *in her bosom* privately to her
         unclasp (as if it were a book with the covers fastened
         between clasps)

I.2   (stage direction) The first scene took place before the
         house of Leonato, and no change is suggested here;
         Leonato perhaps entered at The Globe from a door in
         the stage façade (his 'house'), and Antonio from another
         entrance. See Introduction, p. 23. The name of
         Leonato's brother is not given here in Q or F, and is
         only established in the dialogue at V.1.100.
1   *cousin.* This is used generally to mean 'kinsman';
         Antonio's son is not mentioned again after this scene.
5   *they* (the news, or new tidings, properly a plural)
6   *event* outcome
8   *thick-pleached* thickly hedged with intertwined branches
10   *discovered* revealed
12   *accordant* sympathetic
13   *take the present time by the top* seize the opportunity (an
         allusion to the proverb, 'Take Occasion by the forelock,
         for she is bald behind')
15   *wit* intelligence
22–4   *Cousin ... cousin* (Antonio's son, who leads on the
         attendants and the musician)
23   *cry you mercy* beg your pardon

I.3   (stage direction) The same setting, somewhere outside
         Leonato's house; Borachio refers to it 'yonder' (line
         39). It is supper-time, and the characters leave to join
         the 'great supper' at Leonato's house.

1   *What the good-year* (a general expletive, equivalent to 'What the devil!')

2   *out of measure* excessively

9   *sufferance* endurance

11   *born under Saturn* (and ruled by its astrological influence, making him gloomy and 'saturnine')

12   *mortifying mischief* killing misfortune. He is thinking of his defeat in battle, his being taken prisoner, and his bastardy.

16   *claw* flatter (literally, scratch; compare the modern 'scratch one's back')

25   *canker* dog-rose. Don John would rather be independent, like the wild rose in the hedge, than nurtured under his brother's influence. Compare Shakespeare's Sonnet 54 for a similar contrast.

26   *blood* disposition, and family status as a bastard of the blood royal

27   *carriage* mode of behaviour

30–31   *trusted with a muzzle . . . clog.* Don John likens himself to a beast, muzzled and hobbled, not trusted and not really free; his complaint is unjustified, but the image perhaps appropriate.

36   *use it only* (do nothing else but cultivate it)

37   *Borachio.* The word is from the Spanish 'borracha', meaning a leather bottle used for wine, and suggesting drunkenness. Borachio lives up to his name, as is seen at III.3.102.

42   *model* design; originally, an architect's drawings for a projected building

43   *What is he for a fool* what sort of a fool is he?

48   *proper squire* fine young lover. Don John pours his scorn on Claudio.

52   *March-chick* precocious youngster (like a bird hatched very early in spring)

54   *entertained for* hired as

55   *smoking* perfuming or fumigating. So Leonato's house was prepared for guests.

56   *sad* serious

57   *arras*. Tapestries were hung on the walls of rooms for warmth and decoration, and were often mounted far enough away from the wall to allow a man to hide in the space between.

61   *start-up* upstart

62   *cross* thwart, but quibbling on the meaning 'make the sign of the cross', so leading to 'bless' (benefit)

63   *sure* reliable

68   *prove* find out by experience

II.1   (stage direction) The supper spoken of in I.3 is now over, and dancing is about to begin; the scene takes place inside Leonato's house.

9   *my lady's eldest son* (a widow's eldest son, and so a spoiled child and a foolish talker)

17   *shrewd* sharp

18   *curst* ill-tempered

20-21   '*God sends a curst cow short horns*'. This is proverbial, and means 'God takes care that the vicious lack power to do harm'.

24   *Just* just so

        husband. Beatrice makes the common play on *horns* as both phallus and emblem of cuckoldry; see line 38.

27   *lie in the woollen* sleep between rough blankets (instead of sheets)

34-5   *take sixpence ... lead his apes into hell*. The proverbial fate of a woman who died an old maid was to lead apes in hell. The bear-ward, or bear-keeper, was a familiar figure in Shakespeare's London, where bear-baiting, in which mastiff dogs were set to attack a chained bear, was a favourite sport.

41   *Saint Peter* (as gatekeeper of heaven; see Matthew 16.19)

        for the heavens (a common interjection, especially appropriate here as she is thinking of heaven)

133

42 *bachelors* unmarried men and women

52 *metal* material (but also 'mettle' or spirit, earth being dull and heavy)

53-5 *earth ... valiant dust ... clod of wayward marl.* This alludes to Genesis 2.7, 'God formed man of the dust of the ground'; Beatrice's jest is that woman was made of Adam's rib, and not of earth.

56-7 *brethren ... kindred* (a reference to the 'Table of Kindred and Affinity' included in the *Book of Common Prayer*, and listing the relatives a man and woman may not marry)

59 *in that kind* in that way (that is, concerning marriage)

62 *in good time* (quibbling on *time* as measure or tempo in music)

62-3 *important* pressing

63 *measure* moderation (but also a kind of stately dance)

66 *cinquepace* a lively dance (French '*cinq pas*' = five paces). The word was pronounced 'sink a pace' – hence the pun at line 70.

68 *ancientry* old-fashioned formality

69 *bad legs* (presumably a mark of decrepitude)

72 *passing* very

77 *walk a bout* (as couples pair off for the dance)
    friend lover

84 *favour* looks

84-5 *God defend the lute should be like the case* (God forbid that your face should be like your mask)

86 *Philemon's roof; within the house is Jove.* Philemon, a peasant, entertained Jupiter hospitably in his humble cottage, which, in the account of the legend Shakespeare knew, in Arthur Golding's translation of Ovid, *Metamorphoses*, 8.632, was 'thatched all with straw'. Lines 86-7 form 'fourteeners', rhymed verses with seven accents, the measure of Golding's Ovid.

87 *visor* mask

88, 91, 93 *Balthasar.* In Q and F these lines are assigned to Benedick, but the pairs of dancers talk in turn, and

Benedick is paired with Beatrice at line 111, so that there is good reason to think the speeches wrongly assigned here.

98   *clerk* (parish clerk, who led the responses in church services)

101   *At a word* briefly

102   *waggling* (trembling of old age)

105   *dry* dried or withered
      up and down all over

116   *'Hundred Merry Tales'* (a common jest-book, first printed in 1525)

124   *only his* (his only)
      impossible incredible

126   *villainy* coarseness

126-7   *pleases men and angers them* (pleases by being rude about others, and angers by slandering his hearers)

128   *fleet* company (the 'fleet' of couples sailing in the dance)

135   *partridge wing*. This has almost no meat on it; her jest is to suggest that Benedick's appetite is at best minimal.

137   *leaders* (the first couple in the dance)

156   *banquet* (a dessert of sweetmeats, fruit and wine, served separately as a refreshment after the dance)

161   *office* business

165   *faith* a friend's loyalty
      blood passion

166   *accident of hourly proof* common happening (one seen every hour)

172   *willow* (the common emblem of unrequited love)

173   *County* Count (a common form)

174   *usurer's chain*. The fashion was for wealthy men to wear a gold chain hanging on the breast.

175   *scarf* the sash worn by soldiers diagonally across the body from one shoulder. Benedick implies that Claudio will either make money out of the loss of Hero by demanding something of the Prince, or else will challenge the Prince to a fight.

178   *drovier* drover, cattle-dealer

182-3   *strike like the blind man . . . beat the post* that is, strike out wildly. The allusion is to Lazarillo de Tormes, the boy-hero of a Spanish romance, who leads a blind master about. An English translation was published in 1586.

184   *If it will not be* (if you will not leave me)

190-91   *puts the world into her person* assumes that the world's opinion of me is the same as her own personal opinion

191   *gives me out* reports me

192   (stage direction) *Enter Don Pedro, with Leonato and Hero.* The Quarto adds Don John, Borachio and Conrade for good measure, but this must be an error. Most editors adopt the Folio arrangement, and bring on Don Pedro only here, with Leonato and Hero entering at line 239; but Hero must be on stage at line 198 (*this young lady*), and it is appropriate for her to enter with her father, not with Claudio.

195-6   *part of Lady Fame* (in spreading rumour)

196-7   *lodge in a warren* (a gamekeeper's lodge in a park, which would be lonely, and so breed melancholy)

212   *them* (the young birds in the nest)

214-15   *If their singing answer your saying, by my faith you say honestly* if what you say proves true, then indeed you speak honourably

219   *misused* abused

223-4   *duller than a great thaw* (for then roads were impassable, and people were forced to stay at home)

225   *impossible conveyance* incredible skill

226   *mark* target

228   *terminations* (the sharp endings of her sentences)

232-3   *Hercules have turned spit, yea, and have cleft his club to make the fire too.* This alludes to the legend of Omphale, Queen of Lydia, who made Hercules her slave, dressed him as a woman, and set him to spin. To turn the spit was an even more menial task.

234   *Ate* (goddess of discord)

235 *scholar* (one who knew Latin, the language of exorcism)
  conjure her expel the evil spirits out of her

235-7 *while she is here, a man may live as quiet in hell as in a sanctuary* (hell itself becomes a place of refuge while she is on earth)

244 *tooth-picker*. Fashionable toothpicks were made of precious materials like gold and silver, and often jewelled; hence the need to go to Asia for them.

245 *Prester John* (a legendary king, supposed to rule a Christian country in a remote part of Asia or Africa)

246 *great Cham* (the emperor of China)

247 *Pigmies*. These were a legendary race of dwarfs, supposed to live beyond India, or in Ethiopia. The existence of real dwarf races in Africa was not known in Europe until the nineteenth century.

255-8 *lent it me awhile . . . I have lost it*. This passage refers to a previous love-affair between Beatrice and Benedick, not shown in the play, but suggesting a long-established familiarity between them. Beatrice juggles with meanings; the interest (*use*) she gave was her own heart (double his single one), but a false one (*double* meaning also *deceitful*). Thus she repays him with deceit for an occasion when he deceived her with *false dice* into thinking she loved him.

270 *civil as an orange* (punning on 'Seville'; Claudio is bitter-sweet, like a Seville orange)

271 *jealous complexion* (yellow, the colour of jealousy)

272 *blazon* description

273 *conceit* conception (of what has happened)

275 *broke with* told

279-80 *all Grace* (God, the fountainhead of grace)

289 *poor fool* poor dear (an expression of tenderness)

290 *windy side* (away from, as a sailing-ship kept to windward to avoid attack)

292-3 *cousin. | Good Lord, for alliance !* Claudio claims his new relationship by marriage (or *alliance*) in calling Beatrice *cousin*, and she picks this up in her retort.

293–4   *goes every one to the world* everyone gets married

294   *sunburnt* (dried up and ugly to Elizabethans – who prized a white skin in a woman – and hence, neglected)

295   *'Heigh-ho for a husband'* (the title of an old ballad)

297   *getting* begetting (as Beatrice chooses to interpret the word)

310   *star danced* (so influencing her temperament; see I.3.11 and note)

314   *cry you mercy* beg your pardon

314–15   *By your grace's pardon* (please excuse me)

318   *sad* serious

319   *ever* always

320   *unhappiness* misfortune

323–4   *out of suit* out of wooing her (see line 66)

333   *a just seven-night* an exact week

334   *answer my mind* as I would like to have them

336   *breathing* delay

344   *watchings* (loss of sleep, as we would now say)

347   *modest* consistent with modesty

351   *strain* lineage

       approved tested

II.2   (stage direction) This unlocalized scene perhaps returns us to the setting of the scenes in Act I, somewhere outside Leonato's house; another part of the stage would serve to mark it off from II.1.

1   *shall* is going to

3   *cross* thwart

6–7   *whatsoever comes athwart his affection ranges evenly with mine* whatever foils his desire goes along with (and so satisfies) mine

8   *covertly* secretly

19   *temper* concoct

22   *estimation* worth

23   *stale* prostitute

25   *misuse* deceive

25   *vex* torment. Its meaning was stronger than in modern
      usage.

30   *meet hour* suitable time

32   *intend* pretend

35   *cozened* cheated

37   *trial* evidence

38   *instances* examples

39-40 *hear me call Margaret Hero, hear Margaret term me
      Claudio.* Margaret is to be persuaded to impersonate
      Hero, while Borachio pretends to be Claudio. Thus she
      will not suspect villainy, and the Prince and Claudio will
      think that Hero is mocking Claudio as well as deceiving
      him, by play-acting with another lover under his name.
      Margaret is presented as loyal and virtuous in Act V,
      and nowhere appears in Act IV, where she might have
      saved Hero by revealing all. No one notices this on the
      stage, however, and the difficulties which have caused
      some editors to emend 'Claudio' here to 'Borachio'
      appear only in reading the play. See Introduction, p. 15.

44-5 *jealousy shall be called assurance* suspicion shall be called
      certainty

45   *preparation* (for the wedding)

51   *presently* at once

I.3   Benedick enters in the 'orchard' (line 4), or garden, pre-
      sumably of Leonato's house, and later hides in the
      'arbour' (line 34). On the open stage of Shakespeare's
      playhouse a few property trees or bushes may have been
      enough to suggest the scene; a property 'arbour', seem-
      ingly made of a wooden trellis, and covered with what
      look like leaves, is shown on the title-page of Kyd's
      The Spanish Tragedy (printed 1592). The same proper-
      ties or effects were probably used for the garden scene
      in *Twelfth Night* (II.5), and the forest scenes in *As You
      Like It*, but other plays too have garden scenes, for
      example *Richard II* and *Julius Caesar*, so presumably

Shakespeare found this kind of setting an effective one.

5-7   *I am here already ... again*. The Boy means, 'It is as good as done', but Benedick jokes by taking his words literally.

11   *argument* subject

14   *drum and the fife* associated with military music. The fife was a shrill flute-like instrument.

14-15   *tabor and the pipe* (small drum and reed instrument, associated with festivals and social gatherings)

17   *carving* designing

19-20   *turned orthography* become pedantic in his language. Shakespeare meant that he had become a rhetorician or Euphuist (see I.1.13–16 and note), concerned for flowers of style.

25-7   *fair ... wise ... virtuous*. These are just the adjectives he applies to Beatrice later on; see lines 224–6 below.

30   *cheapen* make a bid for

31   *noble, or not I for an angel* punning on the names of coins. These were originally names for the same coin, but in Shakespeare's day the angel was worth 10s., and the noble 6s. 8d.

34   (stage direction) *Enter Don Pedro, Leonato, and Claudio*. Q calls for 'Musicke' here, anticipating the entry of Balthasar at line 40. The Folio omits the entry for Balthasar at line 40, and, in place of 'Musicke' here, has 'and Iacke Wilson', that is, John Wilson, the name of a musician in Shakespeare's company who played the part of Balthasar. See Introduction, p. 26.

40   *We'll fit the hid-fox with a pennyworth* That is, we'll pay him out for his craftiness in hiding. Q and F have 'kid-fox', which makes no sense, and 'k' for 'h' is a simple mistake.

42   *tax not* do not order

44   *the witness still* always evidence

45   *put a strange face on* pretend not to know

53   *noting* attending to, and setting down in a musical score

54 *crotchets* (both 'musical notes', and 'strange fancies')

55 *Note notes, forsooth, and nothing* pay attention to your music and nothing else. 'Nothing' was pronounced like 'noting', and Don Pedro is playing on Balthasar's words in line 53.

57 *sheep's guts*. The music is provided by a stringed instrument, probably a lute.

58 *horn* as sounding to war, or to the hunt. Benedick, as a soldier, affects to despise music.

59 *The Song.* This, with the music, softens the mood, and prepares for talk of love. A setting for this song by a contemporary of Shakespeare, Thomas Ford, survives in manuscript; see F. W. Sternfeld, *Music in Shakespearean Tragedy* (1963), pp. 106–7. It is set for two tenors and a bass, so would not be suitable for performance in the play.

68 *moe* more

69 *dumps* sad songs

79 *for a shift* as a makeshift; for want of someone better

80, 159 *An* if

83 *night-raven* (whose cry was thought to portend death or sickness)

94 *stalk on* (alluding to a stalking-horse, a tame beast made to walk slowly near to wildfowl, concealing the approach of the hunter, who kept behind it)

99–100 *Sits the wind in that corner?* is that how things stand?

102 *enraged* passionate

103 *it is past the infinite of thought* (in other words, no amount of thinking can alter that fact)

108 *discovers* reveals

112 *sit you* the ethical dative, equivalent to 'sit – note this!'. Invention fails Leonato here, and he hands over to Claudio.

120 *gull* trick

121 *white-bearded* (marking Leonato's old age; see V.1.50).

124 *hold it up* keep the fiction going

134 *smock* chemise. Women commonly slept in their under-

141

garments, or smocks, and the word 'nightgown' meant 'dressing-gown'; see III.4.17 and note.

140–41 *sheet? That.* In Q and F 'sheete. That', but the question-mark makes the sense clear; Leonato asks 'do you mean this particular one?', in effect, and Claudio replies, 'That's the one'. There is a quibble here, of course, on bed-sheets.

142–3 *halfpence* tiny pieces. The halfpenny was then a very small silver coin.

152 *ecstasy* frenzy

156 *discover* reveal (see line 108)

159 *alms* deed of charity

164 *blood* passion

167 *guardian* (implying that Beatrice is an orphan; see Introduction, p. 10)

168 *dotage* doting love

169 *daffed all other respects* put aside all other considerations (such as the difference of rank)

176 *bate* abate, yield

178 *tender* offer

180 *contemptible* scornful

181 *proper* handsome

182 *a good outward happiness* a handsome appearance

185 *wit* intelligence

195 *large* coarse

199 *counsel* resolution

206 *Dinner* the midday meal for Elizabethans, and not appropriate to the time, which is evening (line 36). There are many such trivial inconsistencies in Shakespeare's plays.

207 *upon* as a result of

211 *carry* manage

212 *no such matter* there is nothing of the sort

214 *dumb-show* (because they will be tongue-tied, and their usual banter will fail them)

216 *sadly borne* seriously conducted

218 *have their full bent* are stretched to the limit (like a bow)

224–6   *fair ... wise*. See lines 25–7 and note above.

226   *reprove* disprove

229   *quirks* quips

233   *sentences* epigrams (Latin '*sententiae*')

234   *career* course (but see V.1.133 and note)

241   *Fair Beatrice, I thank you for your pains*. In the first flush of love, Benedick breaks into blank verse.

247   *daw* fool (properly, jackdaw)

248   *stomach* appetite, either for dinner or for repartee. Benedick is struck dumb (see line 214).

250   *double meaning*. Benedick's interpretations are, of course, fanciful.

254   *Jew* (that is, no Christian; charity, he thinks, demands that he love her)

III.1   The scene remains Leonato's orchard; time enough has elapsed for the plot against Beatrice to be brought into effect, but the action seems continuous.

     (stage direction) *Ursula*. The spelling 'Ursley' in Q here and at line 4 indicates Hero's familiar pronunciation of the name.

3   *Proposing* conversing

7   *pleachèd* formed by intertwined branches (see I.2.8). The comic irony is happier if this 'bower' is represented by the same 'arbour' that Benedick hid in.

9–11   *like favourites,* | *Made proud by princes ... bred it*. This is probably a general simile, but some think it was added in topical reference to the rebellion of the Earl of Essex in 1601.

12   *listen our propose* hear our conversation
     office task

14   *presently* at once

16   *trace* tread

24–5   *lapwing, runs* | *Close by the ground*. The lapwing, or plover, draws intruders away from its nest in this fashion.

30	*woodbine coverture* honeysuckle shelter
35	*coy* contemptuous
36	*haggards* wild hawks
45–6	*as full as fortunate a bed	As ever Beatrice shall couch upon* (in other words, a wife every bit as good as Beatrice)
52	*Misprizing* despising
54	*All matter else seems weak* all other discourse seems of little worth
55	*project* conception
56	*self-endeared* in love with herself
60	*How* however
61	*spell him backward* misrepresent him (line 68 is another way of saying it)
63	*black* swarthy
	an antic a grotesque figure
65	*agate very vilely cut.* The allusion is to the tiny human figures often cut in agate-stones used as seals.
70	*simpleness* integrity
	purchaseth deserve. The two nouns form one concept, hence the verb is singular.
72	*from* contrary to
76	*press me to death.* This alludes to '*peine forte et dure*', a punishment inflicted on criminals who refused to enter a plea; heavy weights were placed on the victim's chest until he pleaded or died.
79, 80	*with* by
84	*honest* innocent, and such as would not damage her reputation
90	*prized* esteemed
96	*argument* power to reason
100	*married* to be married
101	*every day, tomorrow* (every day in the sense that I shall be married for life, but the ceremony is tomorrow)
102	*attires* head-dresses
103	*furnish* adorn
104	*limed* snared (as with bird-lime)

105	*haps* chance
107	*What fire is in mine ears?* This is an allusion to the common notion that a person's ears burn when others talk of him behind his back; the thought is continued in line 110. In love, Beatrice, like Benedick (see II.3.241), bursts into verse, indeed into rhyming quatrains.
112	*Taming my wild heart.* She picks up the hawk image of lines 35–6 above.
116	*reportingly* merely by hearsay

I.2	This scene is unlocalized, but returns us presumably to the area in front of Leonato's house; the action is more or less continuous in time.
1–2	*consummate* (once a proper form of the past participle) consummated
3–4	*vouchsafe* allow
7–8	*only be bold with Benedick* ask Benedick alone
10	*hangman* (used playfully to mean 'rascal')
15	*sadder* more serious
17	*Hang him, truant !* (hang him for a rogue!)
21–3	*Draw it . . . draw it afterwards* the tooth. But *draw* also means disembowel, as convicted traitors were hanged, drawn, and quartered, and Claudio takes the word up in this sense.
25	*Where* (where there)
	a humour or a worm supposed causes of decay in teeth. In the physiology of the day, humours were body-fluids, and the thought here is of a morbid secretion of one of them.
26	*grief* pain
29	*fancy* love
30	*disguises.* Fashionable Englishmen were noted for their extravagance and constant change of fashion in clothes; see *The Merchant of Venice*, I.2.69–71.
33	*slops* loose breeches
35	*he is no fool for fancy* he is not making a fool of himself

for love (though he may be doing so in affecting strange clothes)

42-3   *old ornament of his cheek hath already stuffed tennis-balls.* Beatrice cannot endure a bearded husband; see II.1.26-27.

46   *civet* (a perfume much used by gentlemen of the period)

52   *paint himself* (use cosmetics)

55   *lute-string and now governed by stops.* Benedick has turned lover, as love-songs were sung to the lute, a stringed instrument regulated by its 'stops', formerly rings of gut, now more commonly bars of wood or metal placed on the fingerboard.

61   *ill conditions* bad qualities

62   *dies* fades away, and *dies* in the act of sex. See V.2.92-3 and note.

63   *buried with her face upwards* (continuing the play on the act of sex; she will be smothered by Benedick)

66   *hobby-horses* (originally a figure of a horse fastened round the waist of a morris-dancer) buffoons

68   *break with* speak to

73   *e'en* evening. See V.1.46.

83   *discover* reveal

86   *aim better at me* judge me better
     that that which

87   *holds you well* loves you

88   *dearness of heart* affection

91-2   *circumstances shortened* omitting the details

98   *paint out* display

100-101   *warrant* proof

117   *bear it coldly* keep calm about it

119   *untowardly turned* wretchedly transformed

III.3   The scene remains the generalized area or street in front of Leonato's house, for which the open stage in Shakespeare's play-house would have served very well; and there is no noticeable time-break.

(stage direction) *Dogberry*. This is a name for the fruit of the dogwood, or mountain ash, and also for the fruit of the dog-rose, and various other plants; a general sense of rotundity and of redness seems warranted.

(stage direction) *Verges*. The name represents a possible spelling of 'verjuice', the acid juice pressed out of unripe fruit, and hence a general term for 'sourness'. Perhaps these meanings give a clue to Shakespeare's idea of Dogberry and Verges; the former seems to have been large, and the latter old and thin or small, from the dialogue at III.5.32–9.

(stage direction) *compartner* associate

(stage direction) *the Watch*. This consisted of those men chosen to act as policemen for the night.

3   *salvation*. Dogberry and Verges are always blundering into the opposite of what they mean; for comment on this feature of their comic dialogue, see Introduction, p. 22.

7   *give them their charge* explain their duties to them.

9   *desartless* lacking in merit. Dogberry intends to say 'deserving'.

10   *constable* (deputy to Dogberry, who is the constable, or officer responsible for supervising the maintenance of public order in a town or district)

14   *well-favoured* good-looking

25   *vagrom* vagrant
      stand halt

37   FIRST WATCHMAN. From here to line 122, neither Q nor F distinguishes in speech-prefixes between the two Watchmen, and the identifying of them as 'First' and 'Second' is a pretty arbitrary matter.

38   *belongs to* is the task of

39   *ancient* experienced

41   *bills* halberds (weapons like a combined spear and battleaxe, which were used by infantry and by watchmen)

50   *true* honest

51   *make* have to do

56   *they that touch pitch will be defiled* (proverbial, from the Apocrypha, Ecclesiasticus 13.1)

73   *present* represent

77   *statutes* laws. The Folio has 'Statues' here, which is probably a printer's error, but is often kept by editors as an appropriate coinage of Dogberry's.

82   *Ha, ah ha!* (presumably a cry of triumph over Verges, and not laughter)

91   *coil* bustle

97   *Mass* (more usually 'by the mass' (but cf. IV.2.49), a common interjection)

98   *scab* (quibbling on the meaning 'scoundrel')

101   *pent-house* overhang. This might be a reference to the canopy which projected over part of the stage in theatres like the Globe.

102   *drunkard.* See the note on I.3.37. Borachio refers, too, to the common proverb, 'in vino veritas', or, a man in drink tells the truth.

105   *stand close* keep quiet and out of sight

110   *be so rich* pay so much

114   *unconfirmed* inexperienced

116   *is nothing to a man. to* means 'in respect of'. Borachio means 'tells us nothing about a man', but Conrade takes the phrase in the sense 'is of no consequence to a man'.

121   *thief* (used in a general sense to mean 'rogue')

127–34   *Seest thou not ... as his club?* Borachio's images are wild and eccentric, reflecting his character rather than actual fashions, though these were notoriously extravagant; see III.2.30 and note.

130–31   *Pharaoh's soldiers in the reechy painting.* This was probably a picture of the drowning of Pharaoh's soldiers in the Red Sea when they were pursuing Moses (Exodus 14.23–8); 'reechy' means 'filthy'.

131   *god Bel's priests* (alluding to the story of Bel and the dragon in the Apocrypha)

132–4 *shaven Hercules . . . codpiece seems as massy as his club?*
       This may perhaps be an allusion again to the story of
       Omphale (see II.1.232–3 and note), but it seems to
       be confused with the tale of Samson and Delilah in
       Judges 16.17–19.

133–4 *codpiece* a pouch, sometimes conspicuous and orna-
       mented, at the front of breeches worn by men. This
       Hercules was depicted in the costume of Shakespeare's
       age.

141   *leans me out. me* is here emphatic, drawing attention to
       the speaker, and 'is equivalent to "mark me", "I tell
       you"' (E. Abbott, *A Shakespearian Grammar*, §
       220).

145   *possessed* instructed

155   *temple* church

160   *right* (a term of respect, as in 'right honourable')

164   *lock* (lovelock, or hanging curl which was fashionable
       among some men of the age)

169–70 *Never speak . . . go with us.* This sentence is assigned to
       Conrade in the Quarto and Folio, where it seems certain
       that a speech-prefix for the Watchman was inadvertently
       omitted.

171–2 *goodly commodity, being taken up of these men's bills*
       very useful, being arrested on the strength of these
       men's halberds. But there is also a quibbling allusion
       to fine goods obtained on credit (*taken up*) in exchange
       for bonds (*bills*).

173   *in question* (meaning both 'subject to legal examination',
       and 'of doubtful value')

4   It is now the following morning, five o'clock as Beatrice
       tells us at line 46, and the characters are indoors dress-
       ing for the wedding. Much of the fun of this scene is
       generated in the way Margaret rouses the interest of
       Beatrice, almost reveals the plot of III.1, and then
       cleverly diverts her suspicion.

6   *rebato* (a stiff ornamental collar)

12   *tire* (a decorative head-dress, made in part of false curls)
         within (it is not seen on stage)

16   *exceeds* is most superior

17   *nightgown* dressing-gown, often finely made of silk or satin and faced with fur. See II.3.134 and note.

18   *cuts* (made in the edge of a garment for ornament, and to show a contrasting colour underneath)

19   *down-sleeves, side-sleeves.* The first were full-length fitted sleeves, the second loose, open sleeves hanging from the shoulder for ornament.

20   *underborne* trimmed underneath. This could refer to a petticoat displayed beneath the dress, or to a trimming along and inside the edge of the skirts to stiffen them.
         quaint elegant

26–7   *Is not marriage honourable in a beggar?* The allusion is to Hebrews 13.4, 'Marriage is honourable in all' (Geneva version).

29   *saving your reverence* a phrase of apology introducing a remark that might offend. Hero's prudishness, Margaret suggests, would have found the word 'husband' more acceptable than 'man'.

29, 32   *an if*

33   *light* (playing on the sense 'wanton')

37   *tune* mood

39   *Clap's into* let's strike up
         'Light o' love'. This was a popular tune; several ballads were set to it, but the original words seem to be lost. Shakespeare plays on the title also in *The Two Gentlemen of Verona*, I.2.83.

40   *burden* (bass accompaniment, or, as Margaret means, a man)

41   *Ye light o' love, with your heels!* Beatrice suggests that Margaret will lie down (be 'light' or wanton) with any man; 'light-heeled' meant 'unchaste'.

43   *barnes* (both 'barns', and 'bairns' or babies)

47–8   *heigh-ho! | For a hawk, a horse, a husband?* 'Heigh-ho!' might be a cry used in hawking or riding, or a sigh for a husband. See II.1.295 and note.

50   *turned Turk* (changed faith, that is, by abandoning her old mockery of love; see II.1.323–4)

51   *star* pole-star

52   *trow* I wonder

53–4 *God send everyone their heart's desire!* See Psalm 37.4, 'Delight thou in the Lord: and he shall give thee thy heart's desire' (*Book of Common Prayer*).

55   *are* have

57   *stuffed* (with a cold in the head, but Margaret takes it in a bawdy sense)

61   *professed apprehension* laid claim to wit

66–7 *Carduus Benedictus* the 'Blessed Thistle' (a herb much used medicinally)

68   *qualm* sudden sickness

71   *moral* hidden meaning

72–83 *Moral? . . . other women do*. Margaret talks nonsense to divert Beatrice's suspicion.

75   *list* please

81   *eats his meat without grudging* is content

82   *converted*. See II.3.21.

85   *false gallop* (properly a canter, but Margaret quibbles, meaning 'I speak truth')

.5   This follows immediately on from the last scene; Dogberry and Verges apparently stay Leonato outside his house as he is hurrying to the wedding.

    (stage direction) *Headborough*. This is the title of a parish officer with functions similar to those of the Constable, but more limited authority.

3   *decerns* (for 'concerns')

11–12 *honest as the skin between his brows* (a common proverb, perhaps explained by another, 'Everyone's fault is written in his forehead')

15   *palabras* be brief (properly *'pocas palabras'* – Spanish
      for 'few words' – a common phrase of the time)

20   *as tedious as a king.* Dogberry thinks 'tedious' means
      'rich', and distorts the proverb, 'as rich as a king'.

21   *of* on

24   *exclamation on* literally, complaint or outcry against.
      Dogberry again picks the wrong word.

29   *excepting* (for 'respecting')

33   *When the age is in, the wit is out* (garbling the proverb,
      'When ale is in, wit is out')

33-4 *it is a world* it is a great thing, a marvel (a proverbial
      phrase)

35   *God's a good man* (a proverbial phrase, meaning 'God is
      good!')

35-8 *an two men ride of a horse . . . all men are not alike.* These
      are more proverbial phrases; Dogberry's speech is a
      tissue of common sayings.

39   *he comes too short of you.* Leonato means in size, not in
      sense; Dogberry is to be imagined as a big man, and
      Verges as slender. See Introduction, p. 21.

43   *aspicious* (confusing 'suspicious' with 'auspicious')

47   *suffigance* (for 'sufficient')

52-3 *Francis Seacoal* presumably the same as George Sea-
      coal; see III.3.11. Shakespeare is often inconsistent in
      unimportant details.

57   *that* his brain. He points to his head.
      non-come. Perhaps he means to say *nonplus*, but in fact
      suggests *'non compos mentis'*, that is, he will drive them
      out of their minds.

IV.1   As always, no location is given in the Quarto and Folio
            for this climactic scene, but at the end of III.4, Benedick
            and others come to fetch Hero 'to church', and this
            must be suggested here. Claudio has sworn to shame
            her before the 'whole congregation' (III.3.153-5), and
            a well-attended wedding-service may have been indi-

cated on Shakespeare's stage by the use of appropriate costumes, properties such as crosses, censers, or other hints of church furniture, together with the mustering of all available actors on stage. A sense of ceremony is important, and Claudio's repudiation of Hero must be seen as a public act. See Introduction, p. 18.

1–3   *plain form . . . particular duties.* To speed the action, the Friar is made to omit the preamble in the service on the responsibilities of marriage.

10   *inward* secret

19–20   *Interjections? Why, then, some be of laughing, as, ah, ha, he!* Benedick jestingly alludes to the section on interjections in William Lily's Latin grammar (1549, and often reprinted), the standard school grammar, which Shakespeare knew well, and cites several times in his plays.

21   *Stand thee by* stand aside
       by your leave if I may so call you

28   *learn* teach

35   *that blood as modest evidence* that blush as evidence of modesty

36   *witness* bear witness to

39   *luxurious* lustful

42   *approvèd* established

43   *proof* trial, attempt

46   *known* had intercourse with

47–8   *embrace me as a husband, | And so extenuate the 'forehand sin.* A marriage by pre-contract, or the formal and witnessed acceptance of each other by a man and a woman, was legally valid, and so they might reasonably have embraced 'beforehand'.

50   *large* free or immodest

55   *Dian* (Diana, goddess of the moon, and of chastity)

57   *blood* sensual appetite

60   *wide* mistakenly (wide of the mark)

63   *stale* prostitute

72   *kindly* natural (as belonging to a father)

80   *Hero itself.* That is, the very name, if it becomes a by-word for lust; he heard Borachio call Margaret 'Hero'. Through the story of Hero and Leander, in which she drowns herself for love, Hero became a type of faithfulness, and Shakespeare may have had this in mind; see Introduction, p. 16.

85   *then are you no maiden* (by denying what they know for a fact, she confesses her guilt)

87   *grievèd* wronged

90   *liberal* licentious

97   *much misgovernment* flagrant misconduct

104   *conjecture* evil suspicion

109   *Come, let us go.* Don John hustles away his dupes; things have worked out as he wished, and it would serve no purpose for Claudio to stay longer.

110   *spirits* vital powers

120   *printed in her blood* (shown in her blushes, and stamped on her life)

124   *on the rearward of reproaches* (immediately after reproaching you)

126   *frame* scheme of things, plan. Capulet complains similarly over his daughter in *Romeo and Juliet*, III.5.164–7.

134   *mine and mine I loved and mine I praised.* Each *mine* refers to his daughter, the *she* of line 137.

136–7   *That I myself was to myself not mine, | Valuing of her* in caring so much for her, I had no thought or regard for myself

138   *that* such that

140–41   *season give | To* make sound again (literally, give relish to)

155   *given way unto this course of fortune* allowed matters to go on in this way

156   *By noting of* (because I have been carefully watching)

160–61   *a fire, | To burn the errors* (an image derived from the burning of heretics in religion at the stake)

164   *experimental seal* the test of experience

164–5   *warrant | The tenor of my book* confirm the substance of my reading

173   *proper* true
180   *unmeet* improper
181   *change* exchange
182   *Refuse* spurn
183   *misprision* mistake
184   *very bent of* a complete devotion to. The phrase originated as a metaphor from archery; see II.3.218 and note.
186   *practice* treacherous contriving
187   *in frame of* in plotting
192   *invention* power to scheme, inventiveness. The word is pronounced here as four syllables.
195   *kind* manner
196   *policy of mind* practical wisdom
198   *quit me of them throughly* settle accounts thoroughly with them
200   *Princes left for dead.* Q and F both have 'Princesse (left for dead)', but Hero is no princess, whereas Don Pedro, and perhaps Don John, who left her 'for dead', may both properly be called princes.
201   *in* at home
203   *mourning ostentation* formal show of mourning
209   *remorse* sorrow
216   *to the worth* at its proper value
218   *rack* exaggerate (stretch as on the rack of torture)
223   *study of imagination* introspective broodings (compare the phrase 'brown study')
224   *organ of her life* feature of her living body
225   *habit* dress
226   *moving* (both 'full of motion', and 'affecting')
229   *liver* (regarded as the seat of love and the passions)
232   *success* what follows (not distinguished in early usage as good or bad)
233   *event* outcome
235   *if all aim but this be levelled false* if we miss our aim in every other respect except this (referring to *supposition* in the next line)
238   *sort* turn out

155

240   *reclusive* cloistered

243   *inwardness* friendly attachment

247   *Being that I flow in grief* (since I overflow, or am over-whelmed by, grief; *flow* also suggests easy movement, and so Leonato can be pulled along by a thread)

250   *to strange sores strangely they strain the cure* (a variant of the common proverb, 'A desperate disease must have a desperate cure')

252   *prolonged* postponed

261   *even* direct

263   *office* task

266   *As strange as the thing I know not.* Beatrice seems to be about to confess her love, but ends cautiously. The rest of her speech is mere equivocation.

271   *eat it* (eat the words of your oath, deny it)

275-6   *protest* swear

279   *in a happy hour* at a propitious moment

289   *I am gone though I am here* (I have gone in spirit, though I am held here by force)

297   *approved* confirmed

299   *bear her in hand* delude her with false pretences

301   *uncovered* barefaced

310   *counties* counts (see II.1.328)

311   *count* (quibbling on 'count' meaning each particular charge in an indictment)
     Count Comfect (sugar-plum count, a title pouring further derision on Claudio)

314   *curtsies* ceremony. The word applied to an obeisance made by either sex.

315   *only turned into tongue* turned into voices only
     trim glib

315-17   *He is now as valiant as Hercules that only tells a lie and swears it* (mere words nowadays suffice to establish a reputation for valour, and no one asks for deeds)

Dogberry and Verges now examine their prisoners, as Leonato instructed them to do at III.5.45. This presumably takes place at about the same time as the wedding, and no time interval is to be imagined.

(stage direction) *Sexton.* Q has 'Towne clearke': that is, the parish clerk, evidently the same person as the Sexton, who was earlier named as Francis Seacoal (see III.5.52–3).

(stage direction) *gowns.* A black gown was the official dress of a constable, and of a sexton.

2   *stool and a cushion* so that he can sit and write notes. He should be carrying his 'pen and inkhorn' (III.5.53).

5   *exhibition* (for 'commission')

12   *sirrah* a contemptuous form of address, hence Conrade's reply. Dogberry is by turns familiar and domineering with the accused.

19   *defend* forbid

26   *go about with* get the better of

30–31   *both in a tale.* That is, they say the same thing. Dogberry is amazed to find them in agreement in answering a question he has just put to both of them.

34   *eftest* quickest. This is Dogberry's invention, perhaps a corruption of 'deftest'.

49   *by mass* (properly 'by the mass', a common oath)

65   *opinioned* (pinioned)

66–71   VERGES *Let them be – in the hands* ... CONRADE *Away! You are an ass.* Some confusion arose in the printing of this passage in the Quarto; lines 66–7, 'Let them be in the hands of *Coxcombe*', are assigned as one speech to 'Couley', or Richard Cowley, the actor in Shakespeare's company who played Verges. The compositor, perhaps confusing the abbreviations 'Cou' (Cowley) and 'Con' (Conrade), must have run two speeches together. The arrangement of the text here makes the best dramatic sense, for clearly Conrade should call Dogberry 'coxcomb'.

66   *be – in the hands* (let their hands be bound)

68   *God's my life* (abbreviating 'God save my life', a common exclamation)

70   *naughty* wicked

81–2 *a fellow that hath had losses.* He boasts that he is rich now, but once was even richer.

82   *two gowns.* Clothes were expensive, and his claim to own two gowns, or cloaks trimmed with fur or velvet, establishes his modest affluence.

V.1   No indication is given of an interval of time since the preceding scene, and the action is continuous. Presumably this scene takes us back to the house of Leonato; see headnote to I.1.

7   *suit with* match

12   *answer every strain for strain* correspond, pang for pang.
      Strain also suggests the meaning 'tune', as *answer* could mean to sing antiphonally.

16   *sorry wag* pitiful jester. This is the best emendation of 'sorrow, wagge,' (Q and F), which makes nonsense.
      cry 'hem!' (in hesitation or doubt)

17–18 *make misfortune drunk | With candle-wasters* drown sorrow in philosophy
      candle-wasters bookworms, burners of midnight oil

24   *preceptial medicine* medicine composed of precepts

27   *office* business

28   *wring* writhe

29   *sufficiency* ability

30   *moral* full of moral precepts

32   *advertisement* advice

33   *Therein do men from children nothing differ* (in other words, you are being childish)

37   *writ the style of gods* affected a god-like superiority in their writings

38   *made a push at chance and sufferance* scoffed at misfortune and suffering

46   *Good-e'en* good evening (properly, God give you good even, a greeting used at any time after midday)

49   *all is one* no matter for that

55   *beshrew* a curse on

57   *to* (in moving to)

58   *fleer* gibe

62   *to thy head* to your face

66   *trial of a man* (to fight – a judicial trial by combat)

72   *My villainy?* Claudio seems not to notice the news of Hero's death and burial, but is concerned only for himself.

75   *nice fence* skill at fencing

78   *daff me* brush me off

80–101   *He shall kill two of us, and men indeed . . . me deal in this.* Antonio, now so angry, has just been preaching patience to Leonato.

82   *Win me and wear me* (a proverbial phrase, meaning, 'Let him overcome me, and he is welcome to boast')

84   *foining* thrusting (a fencing term)

91   *apes* fools
       Jacks knaves (see I.1.171 and note)

93   *utmost scruple* last ounce (an apothecary's measure equalling 20 grains, a tiny amount)

94   *Scambling* scuffling
       fashion-monging constantly changing fashions

95   *cog* cheat
       flout mock

96   *anticly* grotesquely
       show outward hideousness have a frightening appearance

102   *wake your patience* urge you to forbearance

115   *with* by

117   *doubt* incline to think

122   *high-proof* proved in the highest degree

127-8   *bid thee draw, as we do the minstrels.* Claudio does not realize that Benedick is serious.

128   *draw* (a musical instrument from its case)

131-2   *care killed a cat* (a common proverb)

133   *in the career* at full charge (an image from tilting with
       lances at tournaments)

133, 169, 199 *an if*

136   *broke cross* snapped in the middle (a mark of clumsiness
       in the tilter, who was supposed to carry his lance
       straight against his opponent, and not swerve aside,
       when it might be broken)

139   *he knows how to turn his girdle* he knows he must put up
       with it, for no one will mind him. The reference is to a
       common proverb, 'If you be angry, you may turn the
       buckle of your girdle behind you.'

144   *Do me right* give me satisfaction
       protest proclaim

149–50 *calf's head and a capon.* By imputation, Claudio abuses
       Benedick as a fool (calf) and a weakling.

151   *curiously* skilfully

152   *woodcock* simpleton (from the ease with which this bird
       was taken in a snare)

159   *wise gentleman* (ironically suggesting a fool or wiseacre)

160   *hath the tongues* knows several languages

164   *trans-shape* transform

165   *properest* most handsome

171   *old man's daughter* (meaning Hero, and referring to
       III.1)

172–3 *God saw him when he was hid in the garden* (alluding to
       Genesis 3.8, where Adam tries to hide from God)

174–7 *savage bull's horns ... married man.* See I.1.242–7,
       where Benedick boasted he would never submit to the
       yoke as the 'savage bull' does.

179   *gossip-like* tattling

192   *pretty* fine (in an ironic sense)

192–3 *goes in his doublet and hose and leaves off his wit* goes
       ready to fight, and puts aside his intelligence. A man
       would prepare for action by taking off his cloak, which
       suggested Don Pedro's jest.

194–5 *He is then a giant to an ape; but then is an ape a doctor to
       such a man* he then seems to a fool (ape) to be a hero;

160

but a fool is then wise compared to such a man. 'Doctor' means simply 'man of learning'.

196   *pluck up* rouse yourself

197   *sad* serious

199   *reasons* (quibbling on 'raisins'; the words were much closer in pronunciation than they are now; see *1 Henry IV*, II.4.231)

203   *Hearken after* inquire into

215   *well suited* nicely set out. He means that Don Pedro has found four ways of saying the same thing.

218   *cunning* clever

238   *Sweet Hero*. Only now, on hearing of Hero's innocence, does Claudio's love revive; the Friar had expected that the news of her death would do the trick, see IV.1.212–234.

239   *rare semblance that* fine or lovely likeness in which

258   *patience* (pronounced as three syllables)

260   *Impose* subject

268   *Possess* inform

270   *invention* poetic skill, imagination (pronounced as four syllables)

271–2   *Hang her an epitaph . . . sing it tonight*. This was suggested by the Friar at IV.1.203–6.

275   *daughter* (invented for the occasion; at I.2.1–2 it was mentioned that Antonio has a son)

278   *right* (quibbling on 'rite': either way the phrase means 'make her your wife')

284   *naughty* wicked

286   *packed* involved as an accomplice

291–2   *under white and black* in writing

294–5   *one Deformed*. Dogberry embroiders on what was overheard at III.3.121–4.

304   *God save the foundation!* Dogberry gives thanks as if he had received alms at some religious foundation.

317   *lewd* base

V.2   It would be appropriate for this scene, in which a gaiety of tone is restored, to suggest again the garden of II.3 and III.1; Ursula's phrase, 'Yonder's old coil at home', at lines 86–7, indicates that the scene takes place outside Leonato's house.

6   *style* (quibbling on 'stile')

7   *come over* surpass, and cross

9   *come over me* a sexual quibble. An undercurrent of bawdy allusion runs through the jesting of this scene, especially the dialogue with Margaret.

10   *keep below stairs* remain a servant (and not become a 'mistress')

17   *bucklers* small shields used for warding off thrusts. Benedick says, in effect, 'I surrender'.

21   *pikes* (the spikes which were mounted in the centre of bucklers)
         vice screw. Benedick's bawdy jest is plain enough.

26–9   *The God of love ... I deserve.* These lines, printed as prose in Q and F, were the beginning of an old song, now lost, but referred to often enough to suggest that it was well known.

30–31   *Leander the good swimmer, Troilus the first employer of panders.* These are stock examples of legendary faithful lovers. Leander's swimming of the Hellespont to visit Hero was celebrated in Christopher Marlowe's *Hero and Leander* (published 1598); Troilus used Pandarus as his go-between in wooing Cressida.

32   *quondam carpet-mongers* former ladies'-men. A carpet-monger was one who frequented boudoirs, or private and carpeted rooms.

37   *innocent* silly

45   *came* came for

54   *subscribe him* write him down. Benedick refers here to his challenge at V.1.142–5.

57–8   *so politic a state* such a well-organized rule

61   *epithet* expression

68–70   *praise himself ... lived in the time of good neighbours.*

They are quibbling over the common proverb 'He who praises himself has ill neighbours'. Benedick claims that good neighbours no longer exist, and so men must praise themselves.

74   *Question* (roughly equivalent to 'Since you ask me, I'll answer')

75   *rheum* tears

76   *Don Worm, his conscience* (probably alluding to the common image of conscience as a tormenting 'worm' or serpent: see Isaiah 66.24 and Mark 9.44)

87   *old coil* great confusion

88   *abused* deceived

90   *presently* at once

92-3   *die in thy lap and be buried in thy eyes.* The image of sexual orgasm as dying was common in lyric poetry of the period; see Shakespeare's Sonnet 92, line 12.

This scene needs to recapture the solemn atmosphere of the church scene, IV.1 (see headnote to that scene), and similar effects may have been used; the 'monument' here displayed was perhaps seen in IV.1, where it is referred to as 'your family's old monument' (line 204). This night-scene marks the passage of time to a new day, lines 25-7.

   (stage direction) *tapers* (wax candles for devotional use)

3   CLAUDIO . . . *Epitaph.* Q and F simply print the heading 'Epitaph', and do not assign it to a speaker; they provide a speech-heading for Claudio at line 11, 'Now, music, sound'.

5   *guerdon* recompense

11   *Song.* Q and F name no singer of the Song; it is best assigned to Balthasar, who was the singer at II.3.60.

12-13   *goddess of the night | Those that slew thy virgin knight.* Diana, the moon-goddess, imaged as an armed huntress, was patroness of virgins, who might be called her 'knights'.

20   *utterèd* expressed, commemorated

26   *wheels of Phoebus* (the wheels of the sun-god's chariot)

30   *weeds* clothes. They are wearing black cloaks, or some costume suggesting mourning.

32   *Hymen now with luckier issue speed's* may the god of marriage prosper us with a happier outcome

V.4   A new day brings the return of harmony, and takes us back to Leonato's house, as indicated at line 11, where Leonato tells the ladies to 'Withdraw into a chamber'.

6   *question* investigation

7   *sort* turn out

14   *office* function

17   *confirmed* composed. The word was accented on the first syllable.

20   *undo* (quibbling on the sense 'ruin')

30   *marriage* (pronounced as three syllables)

34   *assembly* (pronounced as four syllables; compare *tickling*, III.1.80)

41   *February face.* Benedick is still showing his disapproval of Don Pedro and Claudio.

43–51   *savage bull . . . just his bleat.* See I.1.241–7, and V.1.174–7; Claudio expands the earlier jesting in this allusion to the story of Jupiter changing himself into a bull in order to carry off the maid Europa. He also implies that Benedick will be a glorious cuckold (*we'll tip thy horns with gold*), and Benedick retorts in kind.

52   *I owe you* (I'll pay you back)

54, 56   ANTONIO Leo(nato) in Q and F, but see lines 15–17 above.

67   *qualify* moderate

69   *largely* fully

71   *presently* at once

83   *but in friendly recompense* except as a return of friendship

87   *halting* limping

97   *Peace! I will stop your mouth* (wrongly assigned to
      Leonato in Q and F)

101–3 *if a man will be beaten with brains, 'a shall wear nothing
       handsome about him* (if a man goes in fear of witticisms,
       he will not dare to wear finery – much less, he implies,
       will he dare to marry)

105   *flout* mock

112   *double-dealer* (both a married man, and an unfaithful
      husband)

119   *of* on

121–2 *There is no staff more reverend than one tipped with horn.*
       This alludes once more to cuckolds' horns. The staff is
       'reverend' both as the emblem of the prince's authority,
       and as the badge of old age.

AN ACCOUNT OF THE TEXT

Much Ado About Nothing was first published in 1600 in an edition believed to have been printed from a manuscript written by Shakespeare himself; this edition is known as the Quarto (Q). The play was then included in the collected edition of Shakespeare's plays published in 1623, and known as the Folio (F). Here it was printed, with some minor changes, from a copy of the Quarto. Many of these changes appear to have no authority, but some add information derived from the playhouse, and a few are of particular interest as reflecting a deliberate editing of the Quarto. At one point the Quarto adds a line of verse which seems to have been omitted accidentally from the Folio (I.1.288–9; see below, Collations, section 2); elsewhere two passages were cut from the Folio text, apparently because of censorship (see Collations, section 2). One passage (IV.2.17–20) plays too freely with the name of God, and may have been excised as a result of the Act to restrain abuses of players passed in 1606; the other reflects harshly on German and Spanish fashions, and is thought to have been cut when the play was revived in 1612–13 in connexion with the marriage of Princess Elizabeth to the Elector Palatine.

The edition closest to Shakespeare's manuscript is the Quarto, on which the present edition is based. The Quarto contains relatively few errors, and these were corrected in the Folio or in subsequent editions (see Collations, sections 1 and 3). The Folio shows many minor differences, and sometimes makes equally good but different sense; in this edition the readings of the Quarto are preferred, as generally more authoritative, but since some Folio corrections or additions have authority, a list of the significant alterations not adopted in the present edition is given in Collations, section 4.

The Quarto of *Much Ado About Nothing* has in common with

other texts thought to have been printed from Shakespeare's manuscript a casual punctuation, and some disconcerting inconsistencies. The dramatist seems to have used the comma as his most usual mark of punctuation, and the Quarto text is lightly punctuated, with relatively few heavy stops, and far less pointing than the modern reader would expect. By contrast, the Folio of 1623, the texts for which were edited in the printing-house, has a very heavy punctuation, marked by frequent employment of the colon in a way now unfamiliar. The present edition is punctuated afresh according to modern usage, but as lightly as is compatible with the phrasing of the text. The few places where the punctuation offers real difficulty, as at II.1.41, are noted in Collations, section 3.

In the stage directions and speech prefixes of the Quarto there are many inconsistencies and inadequacies, such as might arise in an author's manuscript. These are in the main of three kinds. Firstly, the same character may be designated differently in different scenes, or even within a single scene. So Don Pedro appears in stage directions and speech prefixes as both '(Don) Pedro' and 'Prince', Antonio often appears as 'Old' or 'Old man', or as Leonato's brother, and Dogberry and Verges are given their own names sometimes, at other times are called 'Const(able)' and 'Head(borough)', and in part of IV.2 the actors for whom Shakespeare wrote these parts are named in speech prefixes as 'Ke(mp)' and 'Cowley' (see Introduction, p. 26). Secondly, the stage directions are sometimes vague, or incomplete; occasionally more, at other times fewer, characters are named in an entry than have a part in a scene (as at II.1.192, where the Quarto has '*Enter the Prince, Hero, Leonato, Iohn, and Borachio, and Conrade*'; the three last-named characters have no part in the rest of this scene, and clearly must not be on stage); and many exits are not given at all. Thirdly, a notable ghost-character appears in the entries to I.1 and II.1, namely Leonato's wife ('Innogen'). She has no lines, and is not mentioned later in the play.

These confusions were at one time thought to be evidence of revision by Shakespeare, but this theory is discredited. The best

explanation is that the Quarto is based on an author's manuscript in which he worked out the play as he went along, drop-
ping 'Innogen' as an unnecessary part, and not troubling about
consistency. The confusions in the Quarto would make it
impracticable for use in the theatre, where a prompt-copy must
be consistent in names and directions. The Folio text makes
some alterations which seem to stem from the theatre, including, notably, the substitution of the name 'Iacke Wilson' for the
direction 'Musicke' in the Quarto at II.3.34. John Wilson is the
name of a known musician of the time, who must have played
Balthasar the singer before 1623. However, the Folio retains
most of the confusions of the Quarto, and seems to have been
modified by a few corrections from a prompt-copy.

The text we have of the play is not then derived from the
theatre. In the present edition, stage directions have been made,
amplified, cut, or added to where necessary, and speech prefixes
have been made consistent. All this has been silently done,
except where significant alterations have been necessary, or
questions of disputed interpretation are involved; such cases
(like the substitution of the speech prefix BALTHASAR for *Bene*
(*dick*) at II.1.88) are referred to the Commentary or Collations.
The 'long s' [ſ] has been replaced by 's'.

COLLATIONS

I

The following is a list of readings in the present text of *Much
Ado About Nothing* which differ from Q, and were first given
in F. The reading of Q is printed on the right of the square
bracket.

II.1.	76	(stage direction) *masquers, with a drum* (not in Q)	
II.3.	23	an] and	
	137	us of] of vs	
III.1.	0	(stage direction) *Ursula*] Vrsley	
	4	Ursula] *Vrsley*	

III.2. 46 DON PEDRO] *Bene.*
III.4. 17 in] it
V.3. 10 dumb] dead
V.4. 7 sort] sorts

2

The following is a list of passages in Q which were omitted from
F, the second probably in the interests of political censorship
(see above, page 167), the fourth probably because it appeared
blasphemous (see above, page 167), and the others perhaps by
oversight. They are printed as they appear in this edition.

I.1. 288–9 and with her father | And thou shalt have her
III.2. 31–4 or in the shape of two countries at once, as, a
German from the waist downward, all slops, and
a Spaniard from the hip upward, no doublet
IV.1. 18 not knowing what they do
IV.2. 17– CONRADE *and* BORACHIO Yea, sir, we hope.
20 DOGBERRY Write down, that they hope they
serve God – and write God first, for
God defend but God should go
before such villains!
V.4. 33 Here comes the Prince and Claudio.

3

The following readings in the present text of *Much Ado About
Nothing* differ from those of both Q and F. Most of the alterations were first made in subsequent folios (1632, 1664, 1685),
or by eighteenth-century editors. Those of special interest are
discussed in the Commentary. The reading on the right of the
square bracket is common to Q and F unless otherwise indicated.

The Characters in the Play] (not in Q , F)
I.1. 0 (stage direction) *Messina, Hero*] *Messina, Innogen*

        his wife, Hero

I.1. 1, 9   Pedro] *Peter*

      39   bird-bolt] *burbolt*

      82   Benedick] *Benedict*

    189   (stage direction) *Pedro] Pedro, Iohn the Bastard*

I.2. 21   (stage direction) *Attendants cross the stage, led by Antonio's son, and accompanied by Balthasar the musician]* (not in Q, F)

II.1. 0   (stage direction) *Antonio] his brother, his wife*

         (stage direction) *Margaret, and Ursula] and a kinsman*

      41   Peter for the heavens;] *Peter : for the heavens,*

      76   (stage direction) *Don John] or dumbe Iohn*

88, 91, 93 BALTHASAR] *Bene.*

    192   (stage direction) *Enter Don Pedro, with Leonato and Hero] Enter the Prince, Hero, Leonato, Iohn, and Borachio, and Conrade.* Q; *Enter the Prince.* F

II.3. 1   (stage direction) *Enter Boy* (not in Q, F)

      34   (stage direction) *Claudio] Musicke* Q; *and Iacke Wilson.* F

      40   hid-fox] *kid-foxe*

III.2. 26   can] *cannot*

   112   her, tomorrow] *her to morrow*

III.3. 37, 86 FIRST WATCHMAN] *Watch*

44, 48, 53, 65 SECOND WATCHMAN] *Watch*

   168–9 CONRADE Masters – | FIRST WATCHMAN Never speak] *Conr. Masters, neuer speake*

III.5. 9   off] *of*

IV.1. 154   silent been] *bin silent*

   200   Princes] *Princesse*

IV.2. 0   (stage direction) *Enter Dogberry, Verges, and the Sexton] Enter the Constables, Borachio, and the Towne clearke*

      1   DOGBERRY] *Keeper*

      2   VERGES] *Cowley*

      4   DOGBERRY] *Andrew*

      9   DOGBERRY] *Kemp*

IV.2.66–7   VERGES Let them be – in the hands. | CONRADE
Off, coxcomb!] *Couley. (Sex. F)* Let them be in the
hands of Coxcombe.

V.1.   16   sorry wag] sorrow, wagge

       114   like] likt

V. 3.   0   (stage direction) *Balthasar* (not in Q , F)

         3   CLAUDIO (against line 11 in Q, F)

        12   BALTHASAR (not in Q , F)

V.4.   0   (stage direction) *Beatrice* (not in Q, F)

  54, 56   ANTONIO] *Leo.*

        97   BENEDICK] *Leon.*

       126   *FINIS* (omitted in the present edition)

4

The following is a list of readings in the present text of *Much
Ado About Nothing* which stem from Q, but which were signi-
ficantly altered in F. So far as is known these alterations have no
authority, but some have been preferred by editors, and still
appear in a variety of editions. Obvious errors and omissions
are not included here; the reading of F is printed on the right
of the square bracket.

I.1.   89   are you] you are

        99   doubt, sir] doubt

       138   That] This

       210   spoke] speake

       291   you do] doe you

I.2.   4   strange news] newes

I.3.   8   at least] yet

        22   true root] root

        36   make] will make

II.1.   49   say, 'Father, as] say, as

        70   sink] sinks

        86   Jove] Love

       197   I told] told

200–201   him up a] him a

172

II.1. 223 that I was duller] and that I was duller
252 my] this
256 his] a
271 that] a
II.2. 33 in love] in a love
44 truth] truths
II.3. 31 not I for] not for
40 (stage direction) *Enter Balthasar with music*] (not in F)
70 fraud of men was] frauds of men were
157 make but] but make
205 unworthy so] unworthy to have so
210–11 gentlewomen] gentlewoman
218 their] the
III.1. 12 propose] purpose
58 she'll] she
104 limed] tame
III.2. 36 it appear] it to appear
56–7 conclude, conclude] conclude
117 midnight] night
III.3. 35 to talk] talk
42 those] them
77 statutes] Statues
135 and I see] and see
147 they] thy
III.4. 42 see] looke
III.5. 23 pound] times
46 as it may] as may
54 examination these] examine those
IV.1. 20 ah, ha] ha, ha
74 do so] doe
85 are you] you are
94 spoke] spoken
131 smirchèd] smeered
150 the two Princes] the Princes
159 beat] bear
271 swear] sweare by it

AN ACCOUNT OF THE TEXT

IV.1. 287 deny it] denie

311 count, Count Comfect] Count, Confect

327 so I leave] so leave

IV.2. 49 by mass] by th'masse

62–3 Leonato's] Leonato

80 any is in] any in

V.1. 6 comforter] comfort

V.2. 33 names] name

35–6 show it in] shew in

72 monument] monuments

bell rings] bels ring

V.4. 33 (stage direction) *and two or three others*] *with attendants*

105 for what I] for I

READ MORE IN PENGUIN

In every corner of the world, on every subject under the sun, Penguin represents quality and variety – the very best in publishing today.

For complete information about books available from Penguin – including Puffins, Penguin Classics and Arkana – and how to order them, write to us at the appropriate address below. Please note that for copyright reasons the selection of books varies from country to country.

In the United Kingdom: Please write to *Dept. EP, Penguin Books Ltd, Bath Road, Harmondsworth, West Drayton, Middlesex UB7 0DA*

In the United States: Please write to *Consumer Sales, Penguin Putnam Inc., P.O. Box 999, Dept. 17109, Bergenfield, New Jersey 07621-0120.* VISA and MasterCard holders call 1-800-253-6476 to order Penguin titles

In Canada: Please write to *Penguin Books Canada Ltd, 10 Alcorn Avenue, Suite 300, Toronto, Ontario M4V 3B2*

In Australia: Please write to *Penguin Books Australia Ltd, P.O. Box 257, Ringwood, Victoria 3134*

In New Zealand: Please write to *Penguin Books (NZ) Ltd, Private Bag 102902, North Shore Mail Centre, Auckland 10*

In India: Please write to *Penguin Books India Pvt Ltd, 210 Chiranjiv Tower, 43 Nehru Place, New Delhi 110 019*

In the Netherlands: Please write to *Penguin Books Netherlands bv, Postbus 3507, NL-1001 AH Amsterdam*

In Germany: Please write to *Penguin Books Deutschland GmbH, Metzlerstrasse 26, 60594 Frankfurt am Main*

In Spain: Please write to *Penguin Books S. A., Bravo Murillo 19, 1° B, 28015 Madrid*

In Italy: Please write to *Penguin Italia s.r.l., Via Benedetto Croce 2, 20094 Corsico, Milano*

In France: Please write to *Penguin France, Le Carré Wilson, 62 rue Benjamin Baillaud, 31500 Toulouse*

In Japan: Please write to *Penguin Books Japan Ltd, Kaneko Building, 2-3-25 Koraku, Bunkyo-Ku, Tokyo 112*

In South Africa: Please write to *Penguin Books South Africa (Pty) Ltd, Private Bag X14, Parkview, 2122 Johannesburg*

READ MORE IN PENGUIN

THE NEW PENGUIN SHAKESPEARE

All's Well That Ends Well	Barbara Everett
Antony and Cleopatra	Emrys Jones
As You Like It	H. J. Oliver
The Comedy of Errors	Stanley Wells
Coriolanus	G. R. Hibbard
Hamlet	T. J. B. Spencer
Henry IV, Part 1	P. H. Davison
Henry IV, Part 2	P. H. Davison
Henry V	A. R. Humphreys
Henry VI, Parts 1–3 (three volumes)	Norman Sanders
Henry VIII	A. R. Humphreys
Julius Caesar	Norman Sanders
King John	R. L. Smallwood
King Lear	G. K. Hunter
Love's Labour's Lost	John Kerrigan
Macbeth	G. K. Hunter
Measure for Measure	J. M. Nosworthy
The Merchant of Venice	W. Moelwyn Merchant
The Merry Wives of Windsor	G. R. Hibbard
A Midsummer Night's Dream	Stanley Wells
Much Ado About Nothing	R. A. Foakes
The Narrative Poems	Maurice Evans
Othello	Kenneth Muir
Pericles	Philip Edwards
Richard II	Stanley Wells
Richard III	E. A. J. Honigmann
Romeo and Juliet	T. J. B. Spencer
The Sonnets *and* **A Lover's Complaint**	John Kerrigan
The Taming of the Shrew	G. R. Hibbard
The Tempest	Anne Barton
Timon of Athens	G. R. Hibbard
Troilus and Cressida	R. A. Foakes
Twelfth Night	M. M. Mahood
The Two Gentlemen of Verona	Norman Sanders
The Two Noble Kinsmen	N. W. Bawcutt
The Winter's Tale	Ernest Schanzer